TO TOUCH THE FACE OF GOD

John M. Scott, S.J.

Our Sunday Visitor, Inc.
Huntington, Indiana 46750

©*Copyright by Our Sunday Visitor, Inc. 1975*
All rights reserved. No part of this book may be reproduced or transmitted in any form or by any means, electronic or mechanical, including photocopying, recording or by any information storage and retrieval system, without permission in writing from the publisher.

ISBN: 0-87973-789-1
Library of Congress Catalog Card Number: 74-25391

Cover Design by James E. McIlrath

Published, printed and bound in the U.S.A. by
Our Sunday Visitor, Inc.
Noll Plaza
Huntington, Indiana 46750

789

CONTENTS

Introduction — 5
1 / To God in a Space Capsule — 7
2 / How I Wonder What You Are! — 23
3 / Science Puts a Face on God — 41
4 / To God on Skis — 58
5 / A Tree Leads to God — 73
6 / Peace Pipe at Oglala — 81
7 / The Circle of Love — 90
8 / Mother — 102
9 / Three Magic Words — 108
10 / The Language of Love — 122
11 / A Girl Leads to God — 132

INTRODUCTION

Even though you never journey to Cape Kennedy to blast off on top of a Saturn 5 rocket for the moon, or for Mars, you may share, at least to some degree, the experience of the twenty-four men sent to circle the moon or to walk on it.

They felt their consciousness being transformed to behold God making all things new. When Apollo 15 Astronaut Jim Irwin was walking on the moon he was so deeply moved by the beauty of the lunar mountains he felt as though God were walking by his side.

When Apollo 16 Astronaut Charles Duke looked out the hatch of the spacecraft and saw the silent moon rising before him he was overwhelmed by the certainty that he, too, was in contact with God.

You, too, can share in the new surge of wonder

that overcame the Apollo astronauts when they looked at the moon, and then turned back to see planet Earth like a milky sapphire floating alone and fragile in the blackness of space.

May this book help you to stretch out your hands and take the world's wide gift of joy and beauty, open wide your hearts down to their inmost depths, and see that God is beauty, and love, and wonder and enchantment.

John M. Scott

1

TO GOD IN A SPACE CAPSULE

The first astronaut I had the honor of meeting personally was John L. Swigert. He had come to Omaha, Nebraska, for groundbreaking ceremonies at Tranquility Park, a new park on the west side of Omaha.

I was fortunate enough to be in the city at the time, conducting a summer institute in physics for teachers at Creighton University. On Sunday afternoon some of the teachers in my class drove me in their car out to Tranquility Park for groundbreaking ceremonies.

Before Astronaut John Swigert left his footprints in space boots in freshly poured cement in the center of Tranquility Park, he mounted a platform in the open field and gave one of the most direct and heart-warming talks I have ever heard. John Swigert emphasized how the experience of the Apollo 13 astronauts made them realize more keenly than ever their dependence upon God.

Perhaps you may recall the story of man's most perilous week in space, when an exploding oxygen tank crippled the Apollo 13 spacecraft when it was 205,000 miles from planet Earth.

John Swigert concluded his talk by saying, "I want to thank each of you for all the prayers you said that brought us back from the moon."

John Swigert's talk summarized for me the most inspiring thing about our space age, namely: "Space capsules hurtling through space have brought men closer to God."

This flight back to God began with the orbit of the Mercury space capsule, Friendship 7, which took Astronaut John Glenn around the Earth, and made him the first American to circle our globe.

John Glenn's pastor, the Rev. Frank Erwin, told newspaper reporters that if the millions of Americans, who were inspired by Glenn's feat, could only share in his faith, they might also share some of his courage to face the problems of their own daily lives.

In the four hours and forty-one minutes that Glenn was in orbit, he viewed three sunsets and three dawns. For him the words of Scripture sparkled with new meaning: "The heavens show forth the glory of God, and the firmament declares the work of His hands. Day to day utters speech, and night to night shows knowledge" (Psalm 18).

In a beautiful and inspiring talk he gave to the members of his church, John Glenn mentioned that when you look out the window of a space capsule into the great sea of space spinning with millions of sparkling stars, you realize that only a God of beauty and majesty could have created such a universe.

In his talk entitled, "Why I Know There Is A God," John Glenn mentioned that the things that impressed him most are the vastness of the universe, and the clocklike precision with which it moves. Everywhere you look in the universe there is plan, exactness and order, from the smallest atomic structure to swirling galaxies of stars millions of light years in diameter, all traveling in prescribed orbits in relation to one another. The plan evident in the universe is the big thing that proves there is a God with the skill and power to put all this into orbit, and keep it there.

Although John Glenn might not have been aware of it, he was echoing the sentiments expressed by the late Pope Pius XII. During an audience granted to astronomers, Pope Pius said, "Happy is he who can read in the stars the message which they contain, a message worthy of its Author, and capable of rewarding the seeker for his tenacity and ability, but inviting him to recognize Him who gives truth and life and who established His dwelling in the hearts of those who adore and love Him."

It is interesting to note that Abraham Lincoln, the second father of our country, watching the universe of stars marching in order and precision, remarked, "I can see how it might be possible for a man to look down into the mud and be an atheist, but I cannot conceive how he could look up into the heavens and say there is no God."

To the late and much beloved Astronaut Edward H. White goes the honor of being the first in the United States manned space flight program to carry out

EVA (Extravehicular Activity) — the operational term for "walking in space," or, more properly, maneuvering in space by an astronaut outside the spacecraft.

Some of the most dramatic photos of the entire space program are those showing Astronaut Edward H. White orbiting as a human satellite at an altitude of 120 miles above the Pacific Ocean as he approached the coast of California at a speed of 17,500 miles per hour.

Edward White made history in more ways than one. He was not only the first American to walk in space, but, during his "walk" he used his camera to snap the first photograph ever taken of a spacecraft in space from a vantage point outside the spacecraft. You may recall seeing this photo of the Gemini spacecraft cruising through the vastness of space.

Upon his return to Earth, Astronaut Edward White wrote an account for *Guideposts* magazine. Thanks to the kindness of the editor of *Guideposts,* I'm able to relay the story to you. Here, now, are the words of Astronaut Edward White:

"It was shortly after our arrival in Houston that I and the other men in the program each received a very special gift. It was a medal of St. Christopher, the patron saint of travelers. The medal was given to us by Pope John.

"On February 22, 1963," the accompanying letter read, "in an audience with Pope John XXIII, the Pope presented an American emissary with a specially blessed St. Christopher medal for each of the sixteen American astronauts. The Pope volunteered, during this audience, that whenever he learned that there was a man orbiting in space, he said the prayer, 'May God protect this brave man and bring him safely home to Earth.'

"Even though Pat (my wife) and I are active Methodists, this medal meant as much to us, I feel sure, as it did to the McDivitts who are Catholic. I brought it home in its small red box and placed it on a shelf above the desk in my study. It was sitting there at the moment I made my final decision about what personal items to carry aboard Gemini 4.

"When Jim McDivitt and I arrived at Launch Pad 18 on Cape Kennedy, June 3, 1965, I was carrying three symbols, sewn into a special pouch on the left leg of my space suit.

"I took along the St. Christopher medal, a gold Cross, and a Star of David. Faith was the most important thing I had going for me on the flight. I couldn't take something for every religion in the country, but I took the three with which I was most familiar.

"Interestingly, Jim had chosen to bring along his own St. Christopher medal which he had fastened to his instrument panel.

"Once we were in orbit, and weightless, it floated lazily on the end of its short chain, reminding us constantly not only of the prayer Pope John had said for astronauts, but of the prayers of our fellow Americans.

"It's hard to describe the feeling that comes with the knowledge that 190 million people are praying for you and wishing you well: you have the sensation of not being yourself at all. It makes you feel very, very small and humble."

Colonel White's favorite prayer is from the West Point Cadet's Prayer, and reads, in part: "O God, our Father, Thou searcher of men's hearts, help us to draw nearer to Thee in sincerity and truth.... Endow us with courage that is born of loyalty to all that is noble and worthy, that scorns to compromise with vice and injustice, and knows no fear when truth and right are in jeopardy. Kindle our hearts in fellowship with those of a cheerful countenance, and soften our hearts with sympathy for those who sorrow and suffer."

Do you know the name of the first man in the history of the world to compose a prayer while traveling 17,544 miles per hour through space?

His name is Gordon Cooper. The fourth American to orbit the Earth said he offered his prayer, which he put on a tape recorder in space, during his seventeenth orbit in the middle of the night over the Indian Ocean.

In his address to a joint session of Congress, Cooper disclosed that he thanked God for the privilege of being where he was, and prayed for the success of his mission.

Cooper told Congress he had named his spacecraft Faith 7 because of his belief in God, his loyalty to his organization and his confidence in "the entire space team." Cooper ended his nine-minute speech to the Congress with the prayer he had spoken into his tape recorder when he was high over the Indian Ocean.

In this first "space prayer" composed in the vastness of space, Gordon Cooper gave special thanks to God for the privilege of being able to soar through space, and to be able to look out from such a lofty vantage point to view all the startling, wonderful things created by the power of God. He concluded this first "space prayer" by asking God to "bless our families, and all those we love."

Astronaut Eugene Cernan has the unique distinction of being the first man in history to "walk" completely around our planet. Astronauts before him had ventured forth from their space capsules for a limited time only. It was my privilege to share the thrill and excitement of that historic Sunday, June 5, 1966, with Eugene Cernan's parents. In their lovely home in Bellwood, Illinois, just west of the city of Chicago, I congratulated Mr. and Mrs. Andrew Cernan on their son's unprecedented accomplishment.

On that historic Sunday the Cernans had faith that everything would be all right. They attended early Mass at St. Simeon's church in Bellwood before beginning their watchful vigil by TV.

Every day since the space mission began, they had gone to early Mass and Communion. Even in the previous scrubbings (as cancellations or postponements of any part of a space mission were called), when things looked a little uncertain, they kept their schedule of Mass, then home for breakfast, and TV.

On June 26, 1966, the people surrounding Bellwood turned out 150,000 strong for a two-mile parade, and a roaring welcome to the neighborhood boy who came home a space hero.

Astronaut Eugene Cernan did not forget God in his hour of triumph. With his wife, Barbara, and daughter, Teresa, and in company with his parents and relatives, he attended 8:30 a.m. Mass.

Thus, "Eugene Cernan Day" — as it was called — began with a public act of thanks to the great God of time and space who made the wonders of the universe for the wonderment of man.

Astronaut James A. McDivitt, who orbited *terra firma* sixty-two times with Edward H. White aboard Gemini 4, said in a talk at the Foreign Press Club in Rome that he recognized God by His work among the stars as easily as he recognized God by His work among the flowers in a garden.

During Christmas week of 1968 three American astronauts, James A. Lovell, Jr., Frank Borman and William Anders, became the first men to circle the moon.

Sir Bernard Lovell, famed British astronomer, referred to the trip of the Apollo 8 as "one of the historic moments in the development of the human race."

Dr. Thomas O. Paine, acting administrator of NASA (National Aeronautics and Space Administration), said the Apollo 8 flight was "one of the great pioneering efforts of mankind."

In the closing days of 1968 all mankind thrilled to the vision of a new universe. The year would be remembered for the dazzling skills and Promethean daring that sent three men around the moon; 1968 would be celebrated as the year in which men first saw planet Earth from 240,000 miles away in space. As the astronauts made their first orbit around the moon, they looked back and saw *terra firma* silently drifting in a great sea of space like a lonesome blue-and-white spherical ornament for a Christmas tree.

All three of the Apollo 8 crew members are regular churchgoers who take their prayers seriously. On that first Christmas Eve above the moon, as the bleak and desolate lunar scene continued to pass slowly beneath Apollo's windows, Anders' soft voice was heard: "We are now approaching the lunar sunrise, and for all the people back on Earth, the crew of Apollo 8 has a message that we would like to send you: 'In the beginning God created the heaven and the Earth. And the Earth was without form and void and darkness was upon the face of the deep.' "

Anders read another two verses and then Lovell read the following four verses. Borman, a lay leader of an Episcopal church not far from the Houston space center, read the final two verses.

Frank Borman then did something that had never been done before in the history of the universe. He composed man's first prayer above the surface of the moon, the first prayer ever broadcast from high above the moon. "Give us, O God, the vision which can see Thy love in the world in spite of human failure. Give us the faith to trust Thy goodness in spite of our ignorance and weakness."

Astronaut Borman's final prayer and the reading of the Bible were considered to be "the most moving moments of the entire flight" and they were heard by millions gathered around their Christmas trees.

Frank Borman's pastor said the Apollo commander read Genesis out in space so that people could have some rough idea of how the Earth looked to God at the time of creation. A rabbi, listening to the astronauts reading Genesis, told a friend he thought that was how God sounded when He created our planet.

Upon his return to Earth, Astronaut Borman told how thrilled he was to look out upon the magnificence of the universe and see the evidence that God exists.

The reaction to the astronauts reading the Bible in space was interesting. One woman began a campaign to prohibit astronauts from expressing their views in this way. She did get a certain following, because the astronauts received a total of thirty-four letters of complaint.

The letters on the positive side, quite overwhelmed those on the negative. Some 100,000 people wrote in to say that they approved of the Genesis reading, and found it most meaningful and proper.

A bishop in Guatemala wrote to say that in five minutes the astronauts had done more to catch the ear of young people than a dozen committees had done in five years.

Many Jews wrote in to express their thanks that a passage from the Old Testament had been chosen.

Even people who were not regular churchgoers wrote in to let the Apollo astronauts know that they found the readings meaningful.

The letters which meant the most to the astronauts were those that came from behind the Iron Curtain. Letters came from people in Russia, Czechoslovakia, Rumania, Bulgaria, Poland, East Germany, Yugoslavia and Hungary — everywhere, it seemed, but mainland China. Some wrote in stumbling English, some in their own language. Without a single exception, every letter from behind the Iron Curtain was favorable.

It is estimated that one out of every four persons

on *terra firma,* i.e., nearly a billion people in sixty-four countries, heard the Christmas Eve reading from Genesis while Apollo 8 orbited the moon. The three Apollo 8 astronauts imparted to the peoples of Earth a deeply moving religious experience to accompany their excitement over the stupendous achievement of man's reaching the moon.

Upon their return to planet Earth, each of the Apollo 8 astronauts gave fascinating accounts of their experience in space.

Like John Glenn before him, Astronaut Frank Borman gave a beautiful and inspiring talk entitled, "I Saw The Evidence That God Lives."

Astronaut William A. Anders went on to say that it is impossible to view the Earth from space, or circle the moon, without experiencing a deep respect for the beauty and orderliness of the universe. All of us are guided in our journey through life by the wisdom and power of God, who created this universe, and established nature's laws.

Astronaut James Lovell was able to sum up his flight around the moon in one sentence, thanks to a poem he received just before his flight. His former high-school English teacher, Miss Clarke, sent him a poem written by a Canadian aviator in World War II.

"I thought about those lines," said James Lovell. "They were with me through the entire flight. I guess they say what I wish I were articulate enough to say about my experience up there: 'I've trod the high untrespassed sanctity of space, put out my hand, and felt the face of God.' "

Astronaut Eugene Cernan not only had the unique experience of being the first man to "walk" entirely around planet Earth, he also had the opportunity to be one of the Apollo 10 crew that later orbited the moon.

In an article in *Life* magazine Gene Cernan tells how all three astronauts turned to God in a moment of prayer as the Apollo 10 made its final orbit of the moon, and the time came for the crucial rocket firing that would blast the spacecraft out of moon orbit, and send it racing back towards *terra firma*.

Astronaut Tom Stafford, another member of the Apollo 10 mission, told the press that his flight made him realize the words of Psalm 148: "Praise ye the Lord. Praise ye the Lord from the heavens; praise Him in the heights."

It was forty seconds after 3:18 p.m., Sunday afternoon, July 20, 1969, when the spacecraft officially designated LM (Landing Module) 5 — the Eagle — landed on the moon. For the first time in history man was about to set foot on a heavenly body other than his home planet. In this "giant step for mankind" God was not forgotten. Before Astronaut Edwin E. Aldrin, Jr., emerged from the LM to set foot on the moon, he read some passages from the Bible, and received a piece of communion bread, which had been given to him by the pastor of his church, prior to blast-off from Cape Kennedy.

Edwin Aldrin then went on to offer private prayers and echoed his hope that we "recognize that we all are one mankind under God."

On that historic Sunday the astronauts placed on the moon a specially prepared capsule containing a dedicatory inscription written personally by the Pope. It read: "For the glory of the name of God, who gives men such power, we pray and wish well for this wondrous endeavor."

The capsule likewise contained the text of Psalm 8, which the Pope had sent the U.S. government, and was presented to Dr. Thomas O. Paine, administrator of the National Aeronautics and Space Administration.

On July 24 the President of the United States stood on the deck of the *U.S.S. Hornet* in mid-Pacific to greet the astronauts, who had just returned from a successful mission to the moon. The President remarked that the millions of people who were following the exploits of the astronauts on TV most likely now felt that their prayers were answered, hence it would be very appropriate if Chaplain Piirto, the chaplain of the *U.S.S. Hornet,* would step up and offer a prayer of thanksgiving.

In his beautiful prayer, Chaplain Piirto mentioned that our minds are staggered and our spirits exultant with the magnitude and precision of the entire Apollo 11 mission.

"See our enthusiasm," prayed Chaplain Piirto, "and bless our joy with dedicated purpose for the many needs at hand. Link us in friendship with peoples throughout the world as we strive together to better the human condition."

Upon his return to his hometown in Wapakoneta, Ohio, Astronaut Neil Armstrong said that he found it difficult to believe anyone could see the sights he was privileged to see and not be most aware of the power of the Supreme Being and His artwork.

A few months later I received a letter from the Apollo 11 astronauts, Neil A. Armstrong, Michael

Collins and Edwin E. Aldrin. After thanking me for the note of congratulations, which I sent them upon their return from the moon, they continued:

"We are grateful and proud to have participated in the achievement of our national goal of a successful lunar landing and return.

"To those of you who have offered encouragement and good wishes, whose dedicated support has made our programs possible, and whose prayers have sustained us, we extend our humble thanks."

When the Apollo 13 astronauts returned to our planet in April of 1970, the very first item on their agenda as soon as they set foot on the deck of the recovery ship in the Pacific was a public prayer of thanksgiving. The cover picture of *Time* magazine for April 27, 1970, shows the three astronauts standing with heads bowed in prayer aboard the *U.S.S. Iwo Jima*.

When news flashed from the Houston Space Center that the Apollo 13 astronauts had turned back from the moon in a crippled ship, and might not be able to make it back home, an historic, universal offering of prayer took place around the world.

People everywhere began to pray for the safety of the men in space. The Pope offered prayers at St. Peter's, and in almost every country ministers of all religions held prayer services. Many prayed in their homes and at places of work.

Never had there been such a manifestation of human sympathy shown by so many persons of all faiths. They were seeking God's help to bring the three astronauts home safely to their families.

The safe return of the Apollo 13 astronauts is

—Courtesy Wisconsin State Journal (Photo by Father James Strzok, S.J.)

witness to the fact that the prayers of people around the world were not in vain.

On Friday morning, April 17, 1970, when the fate of the Apollo 13 astronauts was most precarious, the *Wisconsin State Journal* did something most extraordinary. Using giant size print they covered the entire front page of the newspaper with this one appeal:

LET US ALL PRAY FOR THEIR SAFE RETURN

The editors of the *Wisconsin State Journal* did more than call upon God in a moment of desperation, they also remembered to express their appreciation following the splashdown of the Apollo 13. The next morning, Saturday, April 18, 1970, a giant banner in red letters shouted from the front page:

THANK GOD

The caption was flanked by a picture of the Apollo 13 astronauts as they stepped from the recovery helicopter to the deck of the converted aircraft carrier.

The remainder of the front page was taken up with accounts of how people the world over prayed for the safe return of the Apollo 13 crew.

It is most encouraging to realize that our exploration of space, and our trips to the moon have been accomplished through the efforts of many men of NASA who make no secret of their faith in God.

Perhaps the words used by James Lovell best summarize the experience of men who cruise the realms of space: "I . . . put out my hand, and felt the face of God."

2

HOW I WONDER WHAT YOU ARE!

If you are a literally minded person you may find fault with Astronaut James Lovell for summarizing his trip around the moon by saying that he put out his hand and "felt the face of God."

"This can't be done," you say, "because God is not an old man with a beard, or even a young man whose face is untouched with a razor."

You are correct. Since God is a spirit, we cannot reach out and "touch" Him directly.

How, then, shall we "contact" God?

Perhaps Albert Einstein may have an answer for us. Although Einstein did not belong to any church or formal religious group, he was a very religious man. In fact, his intimate friend, Banesh Hoffman, says that Einstein was "the most deeply religious man I have known."

Einstein had the humble faith of a child, and readily admitted that "ideas come from God," hence he gave God the credit for the many dazzling theories and dynamic scientific ideas that leaped from his mind.

According to Einstein, the most wonderful thing in this world we can experience is the mysterious — that which leads us to wonder. This sense of wonder and the ability to thrill to the beauty of creation is the source of all true art, science and religion. If we but become alive to the beauty and the marvels of the universe around us, we shall be led to God who is "the most radiant beauty" and the "highest wisdom."

If at any time we cease to wonder, the fault must be our own. The universe in which God has placed us glows with wonder, mystery and fascination. Admiration is the only thing that establishes a kind of equality and proportion between ourselves and the vast universe swirling around us.

We do not understand the wonders of our universe. Gravity, magnetism, electricity and even light itself are dark mysteries. We see very little of the universe. We live in a very small corner of it, and yet, it becomes ours through admiration.

If, according to Carlyle, wonder is the basis of worship, it is easy to understand why children pray. To a child, God lives in every tree. He speaks in the running laughter of a mountain stream. He sketches His beauty on the wings of a butterfly. He parts His hands to let the sun pour nuggets of gold at our feet.

From the majestic Teton mountains of Wyoming to the smiling pansy in your flower box, there is wonder and mystery. Every moment of our lives we dwell in God's wonder world. If we see not the magic, there is no one to blame but ourselves. "To me," said Walt Whitman, "every hour of light and dark is a miracle, every cubic inch of space a miracle."

Those who keep a sense of wonder throughout their lives find God everywhere. St. Bernard of Clairvaux found God in the leaves of beech trees. Francis de Sales was absorbed with the life cycle of bees. Teresa of Avila was interested in silk worms. Joyce Kilmer reminds us that only God can make a tree.

St. Therese, the Little Flower, loved lightning and thunder. After a thunderbolt crashed in a nearby field, she wrote, "Far from feeling the least bit afraid, I was delighted; it seemed God was so near."

Blessed John Colombini trained his disciples to enjoy nature in God. "Just think. We are allowed to live, to walk about in this beautiful warm sunshine, to see the clear, blue sky, and to breathe the fresh air."

St. Catherine of Siena loved nature and understood its sweet harmonies. When she saw a flowering meadow, she said to her companions: "Do you not see how all these things adore God and speak of God?"

St. Catherine caught all the mysterious voices of living and sentient nature. The wind in the woods, and the wild melodies of storm and water on the heights of the Apennines were gathered up by her spirit into a prayer.

St. Francis of Assisi turned with special joy to all the lightsome, beautiful and bright things in his surroundings — to the light and fire, the running water, flowers and birds.

He possessed an entirely direct love of nature. Every being was for Francis a direct word from God. He realized in the highest degree the worth of all things, and had reverence for them as something precious and holy.

He understood God's presence among His creatures when he felt the immovable firmness and strength of the cliffs and rocks; and directly felt that God is strong and to be trusted. The sight of a flower in the early morning revealed to him the pure beauty of God and His tenderness.

This feeling infused Francis with a constant joy in God, and an uninterrupted tendency to be thankful.

Francis was especially thankful for the sun. "In the morning," he said, "when the sun rises, all men ought to praise God who created it for our use, for all things are made visible by it. But in the evening, when it is night, all men ought to praise God for Brother Fire, which gives our eyes light at night. God gives our eyes light by means of these two brothers."

From his hut in San Damiano, Francis arose early and said, "I will for God's honor and for your comfort and the edification of our neighbors compose a new song of praise about the creatures of the Lord whom we daily make use of, and without whom we could scarcely live."

And Francis sat down, and thought. After a moment he broke forth with the first words of the song, "Altissimo, Omnipotente, Bon Signore" ("Highest, Almighty, Good Lord").

When the song was composed, his heart was full of comfort and joy, and he wished straightway that

Brother Pacificus should take some of the other Brothers with him and go out along the highways. And wherever they found themselves, they were to stop and sing the new song of praise, his Canticle to the Sun.

The late Senator Everett McKinley Dirksen said that he felt God's presence in his life for as long as he could remember. He felt contact with God especially when he worked in his garden, and could watch the miracle of a tiny seed, warmed by the sun, and nurtured by water, sprout into a beautiful flower, or a succulent vegetable.

Commenting on the exploits of the astronauts, Dirksen reminded us that we, too, are astronauts. We are cruising through space this very second on our spaceship, planet Earth. Our speed, as we gallop around the sun, is some 65,000 miles per hour, or about three times as fast as a Saturn 5 rocket.

According to Senator Dirksen the whole pattern of our universe is an amazing tribute to the creative forces of God, who works with meticulous detail, and has an intimate concern for each of us.

Hannah Reitsch is credited with being the first woman to fly a helicopter, and the first woman to fly a jet plane, or a rocket-powered aircraft. She is also the first woman to fly a glider over the Alps.

Hannah loves glider-flying most of all. When soaring high into the wide, blue yonder on the wings of the wind, Hannah says she feels surrounded by the invisible but powerful forces that manifest the presence of God.

Father Anthony Padovano reminds us that God shows Himself to us through the many works He created. If we wish to become sensitive to prayer, we should begin our communion with God by becoming alive to the many wonders surrounding us. We should become alive to the miracles of sight and sound, and the greatest miracle of all, that of love.

Our minds cannot reach out at present and grasp God in the fullness of His splendor. Though God is not visible to us now, He tells us about Himself in love letters.

The love letter God sends us is printed in flaming stars high overhead so that all who see may read. It is inscribed in the fragile beauty of the orchid, emblazoned in the scarlet glory of sunset, and sculptured in granite upthrusts of mountains rising to the sky.

Quiet beaver ponds ringed round with solemn spruce, myriads of stars beating with hearts of fire, white and topaz and misty red, the wind whispering its secrets to the treetops — all these are sacramental things to teach the souls of men.

Joseph Addison tells us:

> The spacious firmament on high,
> With all the blue ethereal sky,
> And spangled heavens, a shining frame
> Their great Original proclaim.
> The unwearied sun, from day to day,
> Does his Creator's power display,
> And published to every land
> The work of an Almighty hand.

"Thee, God, we come from, to Thee go." The universe is all for us — that it may lead us to God.

Therefore, fill your mind with all created beauty, so that the vastness of the sky, the limpid waters, the growing tree speak to us of God.

God rules the world. See Him in the beauty of creation; see the order in the world with its laws, the Earth in its revolutions, the planets in their orbits. Review the vastness of creation so that your heart may expand with God. The universe has a language, which, though silent, is eloquent.

The bulk of far-flung continents, the pressure-heavy depths of the ocean, the everlasting harmony of the twinkling stars, the great winds waltzing down from the regions of Chaos and Immensity; the pounding roar of the surf on granite boulders as the great sea smacks his foaming lips; all these tell us of Him who holds the ocean in the palm of His hand, who made the stars, and calls them all by name.

The more perfect and beautiful the organization of living creatures, the more they show forth the love and skill of their Creator.

A giant redwood rising like a monarch on a California mountainside spreads its huge branches to contest the passage of the clouds. It wrestles with Herculean winds in storm-locked nights. It rests in the mellow glow of moonlight on a midsummer's night. It is a love letter from God in red and green to tell us: "Only God can make a tree."

Like the old master painter in the far-away hills who pours out his heart in a symphony of color to tell his love and devotion, the Master Painter and Artist Supreme etches the story of His love for us in every flower and blossom.

When the forests are a mist of green-gold leaves,

and the meadows embroidered with daisies like bright stars fallen from the sky, we love to walk in the deep, moist woods and through the open places radiant with clusters of flowers. So intricate in design, and lovely in pattern are they, they seem to belong to the scented blossom banks of heaven.

My mother took special delight in the unspoiled beauty of flowers. To her they were symbols of innocence, honor, beauty and glory. They made music out of color, and sang of the beauty and lovableness of God.

Each lilac, each tulip, each petunia for Mother was a cheerful messenger in living color to speak of God's beauty and kindness. Each May, when spring came leaping over the garden fence, Mother delighted in the rainbow-splashed tulips. With heads erect, as straight and tall as if by some proud monarch sent, the tulips marched along her garden wall, a gold and crimson regiment, the first troopers to invade the yard after the long siege of winter.

If there were sermons in stones, and books in babbling brooks — so thought Mother — there were odes and elegies in flowers.

To Mother, flowers were the thoughts of God. It was God who shaped the fragile beauty of the rose, the open-faced loveliness of a pansy, and the enduring simplicity of a geranium.

My mother agreed with the poet-priest, Father John Tabb:

> I see Thee in the distant blue;
> But in the violet's dell of dew,
> Behold, I breathe and touch Thee too.

When spring comes skipping over the hills on tulip-sandaled feet, beauty takes you by the hand, and leads you through cool dells where violets blossom like stars, and daffodils are sparkling suns. Around you the magical hue and shape of distant mountains rise upward like an arrow. As you stand in the valley, which throbs with wave upon wave of color, and light, and fragrance, you slip in close to God, having come to Him by the old, swift avenue of beauty.

Our God is a God of joy, of happiness, and love. You catch the tinkle of His voice in the laughter of a stream. You hear His footsteps in the measured cadence of the bolero. You hear the echo of His joy in the lighthearted music of Mendelssohn. You sense His grandeur in the climactic thunders of Beethoven. You experience His lovableness in the waltzes of Strauss. You thrill to His majesty in the epic symphonies of Bach, Beethoven and Brahms.

Longfellow tells us, "Among the gifts that God hath sent, one of the most magnificent is music."

Great men have given their lives to music. Mozart found in music a magic mirror for his own soaring spirit. The haunting, melancholic music of Liszt gleams with flickering flames of gypsy campfires. Brahms' "Lullaby" captures the magic of a child's world, balanced on faith, and warmed in the glow and radiance of a mother's love.

Music consists of sound poems in which some hear the tread of ancient folklore, some the beat of the sea, the passion of the gale, and some hear the voice of some soaring thing that will not stay imprisoned.

Music sweeps you in its arms in the graceful waltzes of Strauss, or swirls you in the fiery energy of the Mexican hat dance. Music makes your pulse beat with strange, brooding, wistful emotions. A melody transports you to a lonely mountaintop, where you meditate and talk to God.

The more we look around, the more we see to admire. From pulsing stars to pushing seeds; from suns of island universes in the sea of God's immensity, to unseen atoms holding all the might of unimagined power, there is mystery throbbing everywhere.

Man does not live by bread alone, but by the glory of the sky at dawn, the majesty of snowcapped mountains, the flashing silver of a mountain stream, the song of the lark, the rustle of tall corn in the breeze, the magic of the maestro's violin, the shimmering beauty of "Clair De Lune" and the dramatic roll of Ravel's "Bolero."

In an ancient Norse fairy tale, you must travel far and wide beyond seven seas and seven billowing ridges to reach the golden castle of your dreams.

To view the treasures of the universe, however, all you have to do is to lift your eyes to the sky. Stars that dot the evening sky glitter like jewels of Indian princes or diamonds from South African mines.

Look up into the Milky Way and see stars poised pale on the fringes of space, and gathering fire in frail, pink flames. Over your head swings the "drinking cup" of the heavens, the Big Dipper. The seven stars of the Big Dipper have Arabic names that glitter with all the fascination and romance of the mystic East: Alkaid, Mizar, Alioth, Megrez, Phad, Dubhe and Mirak.

Flung in generous handfuls across the velvet black of night are gems dazzling beyond even Sinbad's most fabulous dreams. There is bright Algol, beloved of camel drivers; and blue Denebola, and Vega, the pale sapphire. Mighty Rigel blazes with bluish-white, a jewel made for a king! Betelgeuse glows moody as an opal, while lovely Aldebaran blossoms like a pale ruby in the distant sky.

That golden blur of light shimmering just south of overhead is the Pleiades, the seven sisters of heaven, sending forth a soft, sweet radiance. Many a night you may have seen the Pleiades rising through the mellow shade, then glitter like a swarm of fireflies caught in a silver braid.

From rim to rim, across the bowl of the sky glimmers the star-studded haze, called the Milky Way, that ribbon of light woven of flaming suns.

As you look up at the stars, you can say, "You are mine. For us God made these sentinels in the sky. Our Father who is in heaven spread out the dazzling beauty of the Milky Way to speak His message of love."

Tremendous as are the vast bulks of whirling suns that speed down the printless paths of time, they are but grains of sand to Him who weighs them in the palm of His hand, poises them in their sweeping orbits, and balances their massive weights as easily as dust beams dancing in the sunlight.

As you gaze out into incomprehensible distances, let your heart leap with love. Send your thoughts racing out through the voids of space, vaulting over the Milky Way, and dashing over the three trillion galaxies observable with our largest telescopes. Let your thoughts soar still further and higher until they come at last to the great white throne of God.

The universe was made for this purpose only — to speak a message of love.

So much does God desire the love of your heart, that all the far-flung orbits of the planets, all the vast bulk of mountains, and suns, and distant stars, all the harmony of the spheres, all the galaxies throbbing overhead — all these are but a slight price for Him to pay for your love.

According to St. Paul, the whole creation of the world, and all human history, are nothing but a movement of love from the heart of God, and back again to God's heart.

St. Augustine in his *Confessions* asks: "But what is it that I love when I love You, my God?

"Not the beauty of any bodily thing, nor the order of the seasons, nor the brightness of the light that rejoices the eye, nor the sweet melodies of all songs, nor the sweet fragrance of flowers and ointments and spices; nor bread nor honey. None of these things do I love in loving my God. Yet, in a sense, I do love light, and melody, and fragrance and food and embrace when I love my God.

"And what is this God? I asked the Earth and it answered: 'I am not He'; and all things that are in the Earth made the same confession. I asked the sea and the deeps and the creeping things, and they answered: 'We are not your God; seek higher.'

"I asked the winds that blow, and the whole air with all that is in it answered: 'I am not God.'

"I asked the heavens, the sun, the moon, the

stars, and they answered: 'Neither are we God whom you seek.'

"And I said to all the things that throng about the gateways of the senses: 'Tell me of my God, since you are not He. Tell me something of Him.'

"And they cried out in a great voice: 'He made us.'

"My question was my gazing upon them, and their answer was their beauty."

Every moment of our lives we breathe, stand, or move in the temple of God; for the whole universe is that temple. We see the imprint of His hand in all creation.

Each day a bit of magic is waiting for you. A charming love letter from God folded away in unsuspecting places. You will find love letters in the forest at dusk when the trees are all in shadow and filled with mysterious colors that have no name. You will find them in the patient prairie that sweeps out beyond little towns and loses itself in immensely distant horizons.

When darkness wraps its mantle of silence around the shoulders of the world, a wizard moon steps out behind a mountaintop to orchestrate a soft ballet of moonbeams on a silver lake. Then, with warm importunate hands the moon looses night's jeweled scarf and flings its loveliness across the sky. Caressingly the moon brushes back the twilight's cloud-soft hair, and leaves a gentle kiss upon its brow.

As you continue to gaze at "that orbed maiden with white fire laden, whom mortals call the moon," you suddenly find yourself afloat on an ocean of epic grandeur. Then, silently, one by one, in the infinite meadows of heaven, blossom the lovely stars, the forget-me-nots of the angels. As you look, you know you are honored to be witness of so much majesty; you thrill to know that God is writing you a love letter.

"The mysteries of God," said Pope Paul VI, "make man's heart dance with joy, hope, happiness and rapture."

Much of our happiness lies in realizing and appreciating as well as we possibly can the beauty with which God surrounds us. It is interesting to note that art education has become education in the "art of seeing."

How long since you relished the softness of moss under your hand? Or shared with a foraging squirrel the eager lightness with which it leaps from tree to tree. How long since you listened to the wind among the trees playing celestial symphonies, and saw the branches downward bent, like keys of some great instrument?

Lawrence Welk, the fabulously successful band-leader and TV personality, remarked, "The world becomes a very beautiful place if you treat it as such." And it is through this world that God reveals Himself to us! All of creation speaks of God's presence, and of our being with Him.

In her beautiful and inspiring poem, Louisa E. Sparks* reminds us:

You say you would believe in God

*Permission has been granted to use this poem.

> If a miracle you might see?
> Come, then, and walk with me.
> Come out into my garden —
> A miracle's there I know.
> For I have seen it day by day.
> I've watched each green leaf grow.
> I've watched each tiny, tight-rolled bud
> As it opened to disclose
> In all its glowing beauty
> The miracle of a rose!

The "new" method of teaching religion is to present it the way Christ presented it, as a thing of beauty. "Behold the lilies of the field," said Christ; "see how they grow."

Then He continues, "Not even Solomon in all his splendor was so beautifully dressed. If God so dresses the lilies of the field, will He not take even more care to clothe you?"

This comparison does not merely show God's care for us, but it does so by first of all making Christ's hearers notice a lovely detail of creation. Even these fleeting lines are not too trivial to show evidence of the lavish tenderness of the Father. A God who does this sort of thing cannot but be loving and loved.

Educators advise us who are parents and teachers to keep in mind "the attractiveness of Christianity." We are inclined to accept that which is attractive to us.

According to some of the most recent psychological studies, by the time a child is eight years old, his religious attitudes are formed for life, and not too much happens after that to make profound differences. This means that if a child has not been given some feeling for God before his eighth year, it is very difficult for him to develop it later.

It is sobering, indeed, almost frightening to realize that children who are deprived in early childhood hardly ever catch up to their more fortunate peers later in life.

Staggering as the information may be, we are told that the average child has acquired some fifty percent of his general adult intelligence at the age of four years. And seventy percent at the age of eight years!

New knowledge is absorbed through association with things we know about. Each new discovery — each new building block of knowledge — is cemented to something we already know.

All this helps us realize how important it is that the beauty of God should be discovered by young people by finding God in all creation.

Teaching religion to young people can be as simple as admiring the beauty of a flower. When I was in Ireland I had the good fortune to walk through Dublin's famed Phoenix Park with the Ed McGoldrick family. We had just passed the presidential residence, formerly the Viceregal Lodge, where Eamon de Valera lived, when suddenly five-year-old Mary spotted a beautiful flower so dazzling blue it looked like a piece of the sky fallen down from on high. In a rhapsody of delight Mary stopped to admire the lovely flower, whose beauty was surpassed only by beauty in her own eyes.

"Isn't this pretty?" asked Mary.

"Yes," replied her mother. "And isn't it generous of God to give us such beautiful flowers."

That was all her mother said. She did not have to say more. But what a wonderful thing she did. She was helping her little child discover that beauty leads to God.

One of the delightful things I soon discovered about the Irish is that they talk about God, Christ, Mary, and about the saints as easily as they did about their friends, and they took it for granted that you, too, were on such familiar terms with God.

No wonder H. V. Morton wrote of the Irish, "They live in the shadow of God. They talk about Him as though He helped them that morning to bake the soda-bread in the peat-embers."

The new St. Ann's Church in the mile-high, copper city of Butte, Montana, has captured the idea of Gerard Manley Hopkins that "the world is charged with the grandeur of God."

Its magnificent stained-glass windows shout with light and color, as though giving voice to the words of Teilhard de Chardin: "All of creation speaks of God's presence and of our being with Him. He made the world so that He could reveal Himself to us."

The "Smelting Window" shows rich, red copper pouring from the smelter in Anaconda — a reminder that it is God who stored the earth with precious metals for the use of man. Each shining, new penny, each coil of copper wire is a personal gift from God, sparkling with beauty from His creative hand.

The "Communications Window" glows bright with Telstar flashing its messages across the world, and bringing distant people as close to us as the turn of a dial, a reminder that we should all be one in spirit since God is the Father of all, and we are His children.

One of the most glorious windows is the "Montana Window" which shows the state motto, flower, bird and tree, and then depicts the Land of Shining Mountains from the Yellowstone Park area to Glacier National Park — glittering gems of beauty to remind us of Him who is Beauty Itself.

Truly, the universe is full of magical things, waiting for our wits to grow sharper. There is mystery all around us. There is so little of it we can understand. Light baffles us, and so do the crosscurrents of our own hearts.

It is enough that there is One who knows, and does understand, and in Him we trust. And in due course — in heaven above — we, too, shall understand.

A beautiful Koran prayer reminds us: "The marvels of the starry Heavens, the day that follows the night, the rain that gives life to the Earth, the bird that flies, the horse that gallops, the winds, the clouds, the glance of a woman, the smile of a child, the palm tree that bends, the date that ripens, here, O Believers, are the proofs of the power of Allah."

3

SCIENCE PUTS A FACE ON GOD

"The Saturn shot this morning (2:30 a.m.) was magnificent.

"The giant bird in the launch pad stood tall against the sky; it was painted all white with black trim, and when darkness came ninety searchlights illuminated it. From a distance, it looked like the biggest Christmas tree in the world.

"The countdown continued all night until one-thirty. They had a planned time delay and then at two the count started again. All during this time, we were doing our final checkout tests.

"At minus ten minutes, I went outside; for the moment my work was done. At minus three seconds, the engines fired; at two-thirty, flames 150 feet long engulfed the vehicle. I thought it was going to explode. It then started to rise — slowly. In three seconds, it was high noon and the roar of the engines shook the Earth. I was utterly amazed. The night was clear. I watched it mingle with the stars and disappear into the heavens. It was a most spectacular scene."

This eyewitness account of a scientist at Cape Kennedy enables you to share in the thrill of a launch into outer space.

"Manned space flight is an amazing achievement," said Dr. Wernher von Braun, former director of the George C. Marshall Space Flight Center, and the "Father of the Saturn."

"But," continues the man who designed the

Dr. Wernher von Braun
—*Courtesy NASA*

rocket that brought the Apollo astronauts to the moon, "it has opened for us thus far only a tiny door for viewing the awesome reaches of space.

"Our outlook through this peephole at the vast mysteries of the universe only confirms our belief in the certainty of its Creator."

These words of the greatest rocket expert in the world deserve to be emblazoned in gold, and mounted over the portals of our mind. Again and again Dr. Wernher von Braun reminds us of this fact: *Science leads to God.*

"The two most powerful forces shaping our civilization today," continues Dr. von Braun, "are science and religion. Through science, man strives to learn more of the mysteries of creation. Through religion, he seeks to know the Creator.

"Neither operates independently. It is as difficult for me to understand a scientist who does not acknowledge the presence of a superior rationality behind the existence of the universe, as it is to comprehend a theologian who would deny the advances of science.

"Far from being independent or opposing forces, *science and religion are sisters.* Both seek a better world.

"I find it best through faith to accept God as an intelligent will, perfect in goodness, revealing Himself in the world of experience more fully down through the ages as man's capacity for understanding grows.

"For spiritual comfort, I find assurance in the concept of the fatherhood of God. For ethical guidance, I rely on the corollary concept of the brotherhood of man.

"While science is not a religion, it is a *religious activity* by its presuppositions, its method of working, and its search for truth. *The Creator is revealed through His creation.*

"As Charles A. Coulson says, *'Science is helping to put a face on God.'* "

In a letter I received from Dr. Wernher von Braun, the nation's top rocket expert expressed the hope that the study of science would help people "to see God's handiwork everywhere and thereby unite them to God in prayer."

The person who studies science will find the words of Gilson ringing true: *"Science is one of the greatest praises of God, the understanding of what God has made."*

No doubt you have heard of the laser, the fantastic new light so powerful it can zap a hole in a piece of steel, yet so delicate it can weld detached retinas inside the human eye; so incredible it leaped in a narrow beam from planet Earth to the moon.

Dr. Charles H. Townes, who was awarded the Nobel Prize for his work that led to the laser, reminds us: "Science and religion are both universal, and basically very similar. In fact, to make the argument clear, I should like to adopt the rather extreme point of view that their differences are largely superficial, and that the two become almost indistinguishable if we look at the real nature of each."

How true this is! In science we study the creatures made by God. In religion we study the Creator Himself. But it is only through creatures that we come to know their Creator.

Man's flight to the moon began over 300 years

ago when Sir Isaac Newton gave the world the three laws of motion that now bear his name.

Isaac Newton is proclaimed as one of the greatest scientists who ever lived. His discoveries opened broad new channels of thought. He created differential and integral calculus, as ingenious device as ever came from a mortal mind. He proved the universal nature of gravity, and explained the mystery of the tides, the sea's surging response to the pull of the moon. He broke white light down and proved that it contained all the colors of the rainbow. The paper he published on light founded the science of optics. He also made the first reflecting telescope.

Newton figured out the motions of comets, and predicted their movements with beautiful precision.

Over Newton's grave in Westminster Abbey is this inscription: "Let mortals rejoice that there has existed such and so great an ornament of the human race." This "great ornament of the human race" was a deeply religious man, and was convinced that all of creation mirrors forth the majesty and dignity of Him who created it.

Although Newton received honors that come to few men, he had a very humble opinion of himself: "I seem to have been only like a boy, playing on the seashore and diverting myself in now and then finding a smoother pebble or a prettier shell than ordinary, whilst the great ocean of truth lay all undiscovered before me."

Newton is often considered more of a "theory-making" scientist than a "data-gatherer." In case you do not know it, Newton did not "discover" gravity. Learned men had already accepted the idea of gravity, but thought it was limited only to very small, close distances.

In 1665 the bubonic plague raged in England. Cambridge University sent all students home — among them Isaac Newton. He returned to his mother's house, a young man of twenty-three with nothing to do but wait for school to reopen.

The following months of waiting proved to be among the most dynamic in the history of science. One afternoon, while sitting in the garden, he noticed an apple fall to the ground. Immediately a giant idea leaped up in his mind, and shook him to his roots. Could it be that the same force that pulled the apple from the branch of the apple tree was the same force that keeps the moon in orbit around the Earth? Is it possible that the Earth is "pulling" on the moon? Do the planets tug on each other? Can gravity be found in each piece of matter — an apple, a rock, a mountain? Is gravity an "invisible glue" holding the universe together?

The "answers" were Newton's law of universal gravitation, and his three laws of motion on which all our space exploits are based.

If you are reading this book by light from an electric source, the scientist you can thank for showing us how to generate electricity with a magnet and a coil of wire is Michael Faraday, who is called the world's greatest experimental scientist.

Faraday was honored by membership in many scientific societies; for example, he was elected a foreign member of the United States National Academy of Sciences at its founding in 1863.

Faraday looked upon his pursuit of science as essentially a search for God. "These," he once said of the physical laws, "are the glimmerings we have of the second causes by which the one Great Cause works His wonders and governs the Earth.

"The book of nature, which we read," continued Faraday, "is written by the finger of God. He has set His testimony (like a rainbow) in the heavens."

Faraday experienced genuine curiosity and real joy in his whole approach to nature. The contemplation of nature produced in Faraday a kind of spiritual exaltation. His religious feeling and philosophy could not be kept apart; there was an habitual overflow of the one into the other.

In a lecture in 1847 Faraday said, "Our philosophy, whilst it shows us these things, should lead us to think of Him who hath wrought them, 'for the invisible things of Him from the creation of the world are clearly seen being understood by the things that are made, even His eternal power and Godhead' (Romans 1:20)."

"The man who stands to watch a sunset, moves in close to God." These words of a poet are only too true in respect to Michael Faraday. He took special delight and happiness in that hushed and breathless moment of the day when shadows creep out of the sides of the hills, and the forest is filled with mysterious colors that have no name. Clouds descend the stairway of the sky to mingle with the mountain peaks. From the copper canyons of the west they steal the glowing embers of the dying sun, and scatter them in blazing climax to light campfires in the sky.

This is an hour of silence. An hour made for prayer. Perhaps, here, indeed, is the secret of its enchantment, that all creation at this hour praises God, singing of His beauty, and entreating His benediction for the night. At this time the heart kneels; and did all men with one accord kneel too, the kingdom of God would without hindrance and without delay be established on Earth.

In a broadcast to the nation, Dr. George S. Sperti, director of the Institutum Divi Thomae, pointed out that many of the most capable scientists in our free world believe firmly in God, and welcome the opportunity to express their belief publicly.

Arthur Compton, Nobel Prize winner, told the students of Cornell University that science now has much to say about God.

The American physicist Robert A. Millikan, cited by *Time* magazine for his piety, said, "Science has made a great contribution to religion, for the recent discoveries of physicists have taught us a wholesome lesson in humility, wonder and joy in the face of the yet incomprehensible universe."

An outstanding astronomer, Sir James Jeans, declared, "The whole story of creation can be told with perfect accuracy and completeness in six words: 'God said, "Let there be light." ' "

The name of Dr. O.A. Battista is familiar to countless thousands who have read his many lively articles on science that continually appear in national publications. Besides being a most outstanding author, Dr. Battista is assistant director of the Central Research Department, FMC Corporation. He is also very active in microcrystal research and holds hundreds of U.S. and foreign patents on these materials.

In a Telecture (televised lecture) to Briar Cliff College and Morningside College, Sioux City, Iowa, Dr. Battista reminded his audience that science leads basically to the search toward knowing God in things and phenomena.

Dr. Battista said that he had adopted as his motto the words of St. Augustine, "Learn to love the Creator in all of His creatures, and our Maker in all of His works."

"It is through such a window on my soul," continued O.A. Battista, "as a scientist with deeply rooted religious convictions that I see the wonders of God all about us."

One of the many things that helps Dr. Battista pray to God as a warm, loving Friend is a realization of some of the many "miracles" that God works each day within our bodies.

According to the scientists, our bodies are made up of atoms of various elements that are *lifeless in themselves*. Here, now, is one of the *strangest of mysteries*. The individual atoms in your body do *not* possess life of themselves. They are but whirling electrons that revolve around a center, or nucleus that contains the protons. Yet, your body, which is made of these atoms is *alive!*

What is the magic that makes atoms "come alive" and puts you in the "Pepsi generation"?

We have begun to catch glimpses, as through a glass darkly, of the stupendous complexities of our being, and how wonderful must be the God who ordains such order and precision at every level. So many wonders greet us every step of our journey through life that we may say with the poet, "Still as my horizon grew, larger grew my riches, too. All the world I saw or knew seemed a complex Chinese toy."

And it is fashioned all for you, that it may lead you to Him "who walks upon the wings of the winds, and the clouds are His chariots."

The man who is known to have more ups and downs than any other individual in the world is Auguste Piccard, known as one of the most brilliant physicists in Europe for his research into radioactivity and discovery of the hitherto unknown element, uranium-235.

In 1932, using a balloon, he ascended higher into the stratosphere than man had ever gone — 53,000 feet in an airtight gondola he had designed and built. Next, he turned to another frontier, the then-unknown deep-sea basin. To penetrate it he invented and built the bathyscaphe, the first undersea laboratory, and in it made trip after trip to the ocean floor.

As Auguste's son, Jacques, grew up he acquired from his father the philosophy which has guided him all his life: "Everything speaks of the presence of God. The whole universe around us is sacred, because it is God's. Living things, especially, remind us of the beauty of God."

Jacques has gone on to share his father's desire to explore God's wonderful world. Working with his father, Jacques built the bathyscaphe, *Trieste*. On January 23, 1960, Jacques Piccard and a U.S. Navy diver took the *Trieste* down to the deepest known point in the world's oceans, the Mariana Trench off Guam. On the floor of the Trench, nearly seven miles below the surface of the Pacific, Jacques turned on a switch, and sent light into this utter blackness.

"The heavens show forth the glory of God."
—*Courtesy Moran Towing & Transportation Co.*

And what did Jacques see there, where human eyes had never looked before? A tiny fish swimming past the porthole. Life! Life even here in this eternal nighttime of crushing pressure and bitter cold.

The first time I ever experienced something of the fascination the sea cast on Piccard was on a July 4th afternoon a number of years ago, when I was a student at Fordham University in New York City. I had taken the Long Island train out to Rockaway

51

Beach, and, after putting on a swimming suit, I walked down the gently sloping sands until the incoming waves from the Atlantic broke over me. As the great walls of green-blue water tumbled over and around me, I felt as though I was touching the pulse of God, whose strong heart stirs the ever-beating sea.

The world of medical science offers an interesting item. According to the AMA there are now 7,000 U.S. citizens over the age of 100. Medical men can't say for sure how all these people managed to live so long. But most centenarians, an AMA survey shows, seem to be blessed with easygoing dispositions, a quick sense of humor, a desire to keep active, and a firm belief in God.

According to the world-renowned scientist, Father Pierre Teilhard de Chardin (1881-1955), the great object unconsciously pursued by science is nothing else than the discovery of God.

In words vibrating with enthusiasm and joy, Father Chardin says, "Lord, it is You who, through the imperceptible goadings of sense-beauty, penetrated my heart in order to make its life flow out into Yourself. You came down into me by means of a tiny scrap of created reality; and then, suddenly, You unfurled Your immensity before my eyes and displayed Yourself to me."

Chardin reminds us that it our task to perceive God hidden in the heart of the universe, to utter the words of consecration over all the elements, toils and labors of this world, so that they all become part of the cosmic Christ.

In the life pulsing through our veins, in the material elements that sustain us, it is not only the gifts of

God we discern, it is God Himself, our Creator, whom we encounter.

Father John A. O'Brien, research professor at Notre Dame University, reminds us that every particle of matter is aglow with miracle and with mystery, singing a refrain in honor of the infinite Power from whose creative hands it came.

Emmett J. Culligan, founder of the soft-water industry that bears his name, perceived God shining in the heart of matter. He believed that all of creation speaks of God's presence, and of our being with Him. He made the world so that He could reveal Himself to us.

"In loving God," said Mr. Culligan, "one genuinely loves all His creatures, too — all the people of the earth, all the growing things, and also the rain. And in loving the rain, one somehow understands it."

The Second Vatican Council, summoned by Pope John XXIII in order to initiate a complete review of the Church, has some exciting statements that show the sacred place of science in our lives.

"Whoever labors," says the Council, "to penetrate the secrets of reality with a humble and steady mind, is, even unawares, being led by the hand of God, who holds all things in existence, and gives them their identity.

"Faith and reason," continues the Vatican Council, "give harmonious witness to the unity of all truth."

Here, now, are glowing words from the Council that deserve to be kept in memory: "Never, perhaps, thank God, has there been so clear a possibility as today of *deep understanding between real science and real faith, mutual servants of one another in the one truth."*

Rachel Carson, who died in 1964, was an internationally known marine biologist and author. She created great controversy with her book about insecticides, called *The Silent Spring*.

Rachel Carson loved all of nature — especially the seashore. She believed that each of us is born with a sense of wonder and beauty. She believed that our world is full of wonder and excitement, and it can lead us to God.

Just how the beautiful world around us speaks to us of God is well expressed by the poet Joseph Plunkett:*

> I see his blood upon the rose
> And in the stars the glory of his eyes,
> His body gleams amid eternal snows,
> His tears fall from the skies.
>
> I see his face in every flower;
> The thunder and the singing of the birds
> Are but his voice — and carven by his power
> Rocks are his written words.

John Cardinal Wright informs us that if a believer's reaction to the breakthroughs of modern science is truly religious, it will be enthusiastic.

This enthusiasm will have its roots in delight at

---

*Permission has been granted to use this poem.

the satisfaction of intellectual curiosity about the universe in which we live. It will also find spiritual joy in the increased insight that scientific discoveries give into the omnipotence, majesty and wonder of God.

Dr. Wernher von Braun reminds us that we cannot be exposed to the law and order of the universe without accepting a divine intent in its organization. Like many other scientists before him, Dr. Wernher von Braun says, "All I see teaches me to trust the Creator for all I do not see."

In order to be a wonderful person, and live a wonderful life, you have to have wonderful attitudes. We create our lives and mold them out of our attitudes. You create a wonderful life out of the way you think, and react.

A mystic has been defined as the man or woman who looks beneath the surface of things to see what is really there. A mystic walks around the world with an abiding sense of wonderment. He feels an awesome reverence for what is secret or sacred in reality. In this respect, he has a kinship with the child who treads softly on tiptoe when approaching a nest filled with robins' eggs, or drawing close to see a St. Bernard dog for the first time.

Everywhere he turns, the mystic finds goodness and rejoices in it. Like a troubadour, he sings a song in praise of life and love. Nothing genuinely human fails to raise an echo in his heart.

It is not a dream world he lives in, but a world of mystery and romance in which a man takes God at His word.

To the person who is fascinated by everything he sees and hears, the world is full of romance. Life really consists of the number of points at which you touch it; the more points at which you touch life, the more alive you are. The longer the island of knowledge, the longer the shore of wonder.

May you always be aware of what the poet Gerard Manley Hopkins called "the dearest freshness" that "lives deep down" in things. If you lose the power to discover, you lose something wonderfully human, therefore something splendidly Christian.

Let the tide of wonder flood your heart and mind like an ocean returning up the beaches of your life under the pull of the moon. Beauty comes to the seekers of beauty. Love comes to the heart that loves, and as you feel wonder, marvelous things happen around you.

The greatest wonder of all is that even in death we are one with Him who is life forever. Once we discover God in our lives we are eager and willing to share the physical and psychical burdens of others, to help our friends live with gladness of heart, even though they also have to live with tensions that cannot be merely waved away.

At a commencement address given at Creighton University in Omaha, Nebraska, Clare Boothe Luce reminded her audience that life is a long adventure with God.

And so it is. Tonight you may look up at the stars sparkling like diamonds in the sky, and say, "You are high and bright, but thousands of years from now, when you are burned out and fallen from the sky, I will continue to shine in the glory of my Father's house."

My mother led a marvelous life because she was

interested in so many things. Because of this variety and depth of interest, Mother had an eagerness for life that she shared with others, and made them more alive too.

The last TV program we watched together was on Sunday, July 20, 1969, when the Apollo astronauts set foot on the moon. Mother was as excited about this "giant step for mankind" as she was about the new roses that had blossomed in her garden that day.

When I conducted my mother's funeral at St. Cecilia's Cathedral, it seemed impossible that this vibrant person could be in that casket; which of course she wasn't. She was already exploring something else in our home beyond the stars.

We may conclude this chapter with an Indian prayer:

O Great Spirit, whose voice I hear in the winds, and whose breath gives life to all the world, hear me! I am small and weak, I need Your strength and wisdom.

Let me walk in beauty, and make my eyes ever behold the red and purple sunset.

Make my hands respect the things You have made and my ears sharp to hear Your voice.

Let me learn the lessons You have hidden in every leaf and rock.

Make me always ready to come to You with clean hands and straight eyes.

So when life fades, as the fading sunset, my spirit may come to You without shame.

4

TO GOD ON SKIS

Do you know that the beauty and majesty of the mountains brought one of the world's most famous skiers into the Catholic Church?

Sir Arnold Lunn is the man credited for making skiing the popular sport it now is. In fact, Lunn's knighthood was bestowed upon him by the British queen for his contribution to skiing and to Anglo-Swiss relations.

Sir Arnold invented slalom, the zigzag descent between obstacles. He organized the world's first international downhill ski races, and got the sport into the Olympic program.

An Olympic official once said that if skiing had a pope, Lunn would be it. A bust of Sir Arnold stands in the Ski Club of Great Britain in London.

When he was a young man, Arnold Lunn spent

much time in the Alps. Mountain-climbing and skiing were his two favorite sports. The great towering mountains, the Matterhorn, the Monch and Monte Rosa, rising like arrows to the lofty sky, became his Bible through which he approached the everlasting Architect of the hills. His ideal became that of the mountaineer.

He described the sheen of distant snowfields glistening in the sun, the sweep of forests, the celestial radiance of summits. He counseled the young to leave the "exile" of the plains and go to the heights.

Sir Arnold is a witty, persuasive writer. In America his most popular book is *The Swiss and Their Mountains.* He has been visiting Apologetics Professor at Notre Dame, and gave the Lowell lectures at Harvard. He has written fifty-six books, some of which ran into fifteen printings.

Under the spell of mountain beauty, Lunn broke with materialism and turned to Him who dug the foundations for the massive mountains, and who balances them in the hollow of His hand.

At the age of forty-five, Lunn was admitted into the Catholic Church by Monsignor Ronald Knox, famous translator and author.

Lunn published *Come What May* — a sort of autobiographical *Now See Me,* in which he stresses his experiences in the mountains. For Lunn the Alpine world held an attraction which sometimes became religious.

My first adventure into the high places of the Alps left me breathless with wonder and admiration. As I looked at majestic mountains leaping into the sky, like Saturn 5 rockets, I realized that the Alps are

Valentines from God trimmed in the white lace of snow, and dazzling with diamonds of glittering ice.

The words I had said at the beginning of Mass that morning took on fresh meaning, like words heard for the first time. "Send forth Thy light and Thy truth. They have led me and brought me into Your holy mountain, and into Your tabernacle."

Truly, this was a holy spot. Here, indeed, all of nature sings of God. The words of Psalm 103 leaped into my mind; "O Lord, my God, Thou art exceedingly great. Thou hast put on praise and beauty; and art clothed with light as with a garment. Who makest the clouds Thy chariots; who walks upon the wings of the winds. How great are Thy works, O Lord. Thou hast made all things in wisdom."

The very rocks seemed to echo the words of Psalm 99: "Sing joyfully to God, all the Earth; serve ye the Lord with gladness. Come in before His presence with exceeding great joy."

Here was happiness and delight. Here the vision of a day that would remain forever bright and shining. I could not add one word to all the lyric lines that tell the story of this mystic land.

Now I knew why Pope Pius XI had returned to climb the Alps every summer for almost twenty-eight years.

Pope Pius XI was one of the greatest mountain climbers of this century. On his accession to the throne of St. Peter he was hailed as the Alpinist Pope. Climbing was his chief recreation. No previous Pope has been so distinguished for the exacting athletic ability required in scaling the vertical crags of the Alps at an altitude of 15,000 feet.

Pope Pius XI had come by environment and by bent to love mountaineering. To him, the mountains meant loftiness for both body and soul. Every summer for twenty-eight years, with but three interruptions when he traveled in Italy and Northern Europe, this learned priest climbed the Alps. During that period he made more than 200 ascents, which included those of Mt. Blanc, the highest peak in Europe, Monte Rosa and the Matterhorn.

On the other side of planet Earth, on top of the frigid, windswept heights of the most massive mountain in the world, Mt. Everest, are two "thank you" offerings to God. Two very different gifts offered on the peak of Mt. Everest to Him whose fingers formed the towering heights, and balanced their awful weight.

Tenzing Norgay, the famous Nepalese Sherpa mountaineer, who together with Sir Edmund Hillary scaled the hitherto unconquered Mt. Everest, was interviewed by Father Vincent Gnanapragasm, a Jesuit missionary in India.

"What was the offering you made on the top of Everest?" questioned Father Gnanapragasm.

"Oh! that," Tenzing replied with a smile, as a certain amount of shyness suffused his face. "Well, Father, I took whatever I could lay my hands upon at that moment — a few sweets and chocolate bars — and offered them to the God who made that mountain."

"I remembered," Father Gnanapragasm later stated, "that another offering had been made at that time on the top of the world's greatest peak. Beside the offering made by Tenzing lies a crucifix. It was placed there by Sir Edmund Hillary at the request of Sir John Hunt, the expedition's leader, who had received it from an English priest. There is something symbolic in those two different offerings on the world's nearest point to heaven."

These offerings are a realization of the words of the Royal Psalmist, King David. "Come into the presence of God with thanksgiving; for the Lord is a great God, and a great King above all. For in His hands are all the ends of the Earth; and the heights of the mountains are His; and His hands formed the dry land."

As is evident from reading the Gospels, Christ loved the mountains. Their vastness, their solitude, their mystery and grandeur spun a web of enchantment about Him. From the towering heights of Carmel to the deep gorges of the mountains of Manassas there was beauty and grandeur on every side. The wind brooding its secrets in the treetops was music to His soul. No wonder we read in Scripture that "Christ went up into the mountain to pray."

While speaking of some of the most beautiful mountains in all Ireland — the Mountains of Mourne, H.V. Morton is his book, *In Search Of Ireland,* remarks: "There is a curious dream-like quality about all Irish mountains. Something about them that uplifts the spirit."

He refers to the "unearthly quality" of the Irish landscape which seems half in this world and half in the next. In reference to this "mystical beauty which exists in the high places in Ireland," H.V. Morton says, "I have often wondered during my travels in Ireland whether this country would have produced so many saints had she been a flat, practical land like Holland."

Mountains have always fascinated man, drawing him ever onward and upward. Men have gone to the mountains for many reasons . . . to build a new home and a new life . . . to find and carry away their hidden riches . . . to find peace . . . just to get to the other side.

Men have risked life and limb to climb the highest mountains — again for many reasons. The simplest and at the same time, most complicated: "Because they are there."

In America, the mountains are certainly there. Ages old, the Appalachian range stretches from Maine to Georgia. The younger Rockies, running from New Mexico through Montana, divide the continent. And the youngest of them all, the Sierra Nevada, rears up from California to Oregon.

Alaska boasts two mountain ranges within its borders, as well as North America's tallest peak, Mt. McKinley, 20,320 feet.

In a sense, Hawaii is all mountains, thrust up by volcanic action millions of years ago. The process is still going on, as volcanoes are still building toward the surface of the sea.

America's mountains have helped mold American history in many ways. They were the frontiers beyond which few dared venture until braver, hardier men showed the way. They played a major role in determining how the nation was settled. The mountain men who opened the way west inspired others to follow. Perhaps more important, their courage and strength and love of freedom still inspire Americans of the twentieth century. The motto of one of our mountain states is: "Mountaineers are always free men."

Mountains have molded man and shaped much of his history. The mountains have afforded a refuge to him; always they have been a challenge.

Carved in stone on one of the state buildings in Sacramento, California, are these words: "Bring me men to match my mountains."

A little more than a century ago, Sacramento was the center of modern man's most famous mass move to the mountains, the gold rush of '49.

The men who forced their way to this golden land found in their path an awesome barrier, a great chain of mountain ranges glinting with some of the highest peaks in the country.

In the center there was the Sierra Nevada, a gigantic block of the earth's crust rising like a wall above the plain. Soaring up to 11,000 feet beyond the alkali wastes, its mighty escarpments cast long shadows on the eastern desert, its glistening sawtooth profile unbroken for 430 miles by any bisecting river, canyon or low pass.

In the north the Cascade Range merges its snowy volcanic peaks with the Sierra Nevada. To the south are the Tehachapi, San Gabriel, San Jacinto and Santa Rosa mountain ranges — lower in altitude but formidable in the extreme to cross, especially with the vast southern deserts guarding their approaches.

Small wonder, then, that California was first settled from the sea or from the north or coastal south. But in 1771 Father Francisco Garces, traveling and living like an Indian, broke trail across the Colorado Desert as far as the present Imperial Valley. Then, in 1774 he and Juan Bautista de Anza pushed clear into Mission San Gabriel.

Two years later another priest, Father Pedro Font, accompanying Anza's second expedition, unwittingly gave a name to the greatest of the mountain barriers: the Sierra Nevada.

Standing on the hills east of San Francisco Bay, the missionary beheld in the distance *una gran sierra nevada* — a great snowy range. His descriptive phrase rapidly became a name.

The Sierra Nevada in unbroken length and loftiness of its peaks rivals the Rocky Mountains. The highest of the Sierra peaks is Mt. Whitney (14,496 feet high). Until the annexation of Alaska, Mt. Whitney was the highest peak in the United States.

The Sierra peaks capture prodigious amounts of rain and snow from moist ocean winds. Their eastern walls are cut by short, steep streams; their western slopes carry off large quantities of water in rivers that have carved magnificent canyons.

During July of 1972 I had the good fortune of visiting Yosemite National Park and the High Sierras of California. I promptly fell under the fascination of one of the world's greatest scenic wonders.

Many mountains are like sleeping giants sprawled out across the horizon. You come to the foot of the mountain first, but the top may be still far distant, reached by a long slope of hills and forests that rise more or less leisurely to the summit. You can look at the top of the mountain without leaning back your head.

But in Yosemite, when you come to the foot of a mountain, you find the giant standing upright on his feet, his broad shoulders cutting a solid block against the blue sky. To see the brow of the mountain, you may have to lean your head back and squint up into the heavens.

On Thursday morning, July 20, I stood on the shore of Mirror Lake and looked up at Half Dome, a sheer wall of rock rising almost one mile vertically into the sky. Beams of the late morning sunlight fell around the shoulders of this giant like ermine robes of a mighty emperor.

Half Dome is a mountain of stone that looks like a giant-size loaf of bread sliced in half. The super-size knife that nature used for the cutting edge to slice off half the mountain was the glaciers of thousands of years ago.

On Saturday morning, July 22, when I walked from Yosemite Lodge to El Capitan, I emerged from a belt of trees to stand in silent awe at the most massive wall of exposed granite in the world.

El Capitan stood proud and straight before me like a military hero standing guard over the entrance to the valley. I had to lean my head back to see the sun gleaming from the brow of El Capitan 3,564 feet above me.

Yosemite is a ballet of mountains standing on tiptoe. It is a symphony in stone with sentinel peaks rising like exclamation points in surprise over their own agility. It is a rhapsody of delight in granite monoliths that soar into the zenith as though they never heard of the law of gravity.

On my first day in Yosemite, while walking

along the shore of Mirror Lake, I met a wonderful young man and his family fishing in the ice-cold waters near the foot of Half Dome. The gentleman was John St. John, a policeman from the Los Angeles area. His urbanity, compassion and depth of understanding made me feel happy to realize that our forces of law and order were being represented by such an outstanding man of high ideals.

On my last afternoon in Yosemite, John and his family invited me to ride with them in their car up the mountain road that led to Glacier Point.

We had to park the car about a tenth of a mile from the Point, and then climb a brisk rise to the rim. The sight that exploded before us took our breath in surprise. Straight down from our shoelaces the valley dropped 3,000 feet. Across the valley Half Dome humped its shoulders against the sky. Far in the distance, behind Half Dome, rose the 13,000-foot, snowcapped peaks of the High Sierra, which John Muir called "The Range of Light."

The view from Glacier Point is considered to be one of the most magnificent panoramas in the world. Far to the left was Yosemite Falls, the highest in North America, and second highest in the world, plunging a total of 2,425 feet. Far to the right were Vernal and Nevada Falls — all pageants of free-leaping water. Nowhere in the world are so many and such beautiful and varied waterfalls as in Yosemite.

Yosemite Valley is one of the great geological phenomena of the earth. There is not only beauty here but magic. From snowcapped mountaintops in the distant High Sierra to the leaping falls cascading into the valley, the whole scene sings the praises of the Supreme Being who made such surpassing beauty.

The mountains are a living Bible shouting with joy to the Lord who laid their foundations. They give voice to Psalm 97: "The mountains shall rejoice together at the presence of the Lord."

It was my wonderful good fortune to have grown up in the Land of the Big Sky, or the Land of Shining Mountains, as the state of Montana is called.

The mile-high, copper-mining city of Butte, nestled in the heart of the Rockies, is my hometown. From the front porch of our home at 1139 West Caledonia Street, we commanded a superb view of the surrounding hills that girdled the mining city with an irregular but nearly circular chain of mountains. The mountains surrounding Butte are truly "breathtaking" — as visitors from "back East" find out when they climb up to the peaks. The thin air makes them gasp for oxygen.

The last time I visited Butte, I enjoyed once again the thrill that was mine many times as a boy. I climbed the steep hill back of our home that is known as Big Butte. It is the core of an ancient volcano that once leaped to the sky, and cascaded molten lava over the landscape.

The view you may enjoy from the top of Big Butte is unique. Look east to the other side of the city, and there is the backbone of the Rocky Mountains — the Continental Divide. To the south of the main Divide swings a pair of rugged spurs known as the Highlands.

Look twenty-six miles straight west and you will see the tallest smokestack in the western hemisphere soaring skyward from the smelter at Anaconda. Best of all, you will see the encircling ring of majestic mountains whose snowcapped summits lift their massive shoulders among, and above the clouds.

As I gazed out from the top of Big Butte, I was stabbed with thrust after thrust of wonder and delight, deep, fierce, beautiful.

Here was a magnificent country strong and free as the roving winds; untamed and vigorous as a golden-maned palomino stallion racing with the breeze.

Here was a mighty land, broken and tumbled by a powerful hand. Peak stood on peak, and canyon walls rose to peer over their neighbors.

Here was a symphony in rock and stone shimmering to glittering cadenzas, rumbling to deep bass kettle drums. An ocean of motion caught and held forever in sheer uplifts of granite.

The very air was opalescent as a jewel. Far overhead the sky opened up like a soft blue flower. I felt as though I were soaring on the splendid golden wings of morning and heard the wind whistle my name. And after that, a silence, and a thousand heartbeats of motion.

I thought of that first message Samuel Morse sent racing through telegraph wires, "What hath God wrought?"

Here, indeed, was an answer. Mighty mountains leaping to the sky spoke with a voice of thunder of God's power, His majesty, His grandeur.

How appropriate were the words of Psalm 103, "O Lord my God, Thou art exceedingly great. Thou hast put on praise and beauty; and art clothed with light as with a garment. Who makest the clouds Thy chariot; who walks on the wings of the winds. How great are Thy works, O Lord. Thou hast made all things in wisdom."

The three most wonderful summers of my youth were those I spent with my grandparents, who lived high in the massive mountains back of Buxton, some miles to the west and south of Butte.

In August 1971 I was able to make a return visit to my grandparents' former mountain home. The last portion of the twisting dirt road that leads up to our old log cabin perched on the side of the mountain is washed-out, and so, I made the last portion of the trip on foot.

It was like walking back into a beautiful dream. I heard the wind whispering its secrets to the pines in the treetops. I saw the branches downward bent, like keys of some great instrument. The symphony of the wind among the pines is beyond compare. Its melody is ever gentle on your mind. It holds you captured by its magic spell. The soft, clean sound washes over you with waves of refreshment. You inhale the sparkling air, like an elixir of delight. The air enters your lungs like a rapture. I thought of the words of the "Poet-Priest of the South," Father Abram J. Ryan:

> I walk down the Valley of Silence —
> Down the dim, voiceless Valley — alone!
> And I hear not the fall of a footstep
> Around me, save God's and my own.
>
> In the hush of the Valley of Silence
> I dream all the songs that I sing;
> And the music floats down the dim Valley,

Till each finds a word for a wing,
That to hearts, like the dove of the Deluge,
A message of Peace they may bring.

But far on the deep there are billows
That shall never break on the beach;
And I have heard songs in the Silence
That never shall float into speech;
And I have had dreams in the Valley
Too lofty for language to reach.

I stopped for a moment to enjoy the beauty of the moment, and to fold away a warm and tender memory to cherish forever. The silence I heard around me was the sound of tomorrow taking its time.

My path now took me parallel to a stand of giant pines. As a boy I delighted walking on the thick mat of pine needles that covered the floor of the forest. As always, the mysterious depths of the forest glowed with magic colors that have no name. Once again I stepped on the resilient carpet of pine needles, and felt as though I were walking on a soft, fluffy cloud.

When I reached the front door of our now-deserted cabin, I turned around and looked back over the country I had just traveled. It was a sight to launch a poet into ecstasy. Far on the distant horizon gleamed the lofty peaks of the Continental Divide. On the south side of the wide valley was a thin, black line — the tracks of the Union Pacific heading south for Idaho.

Beaten by a thousand fierce suns, the face of the

valley in late summer was tough and dry. A sudden whirling dervish spun powder-dry dust through the sagebrush, then took to the horizon to whirl through mesas of space wild and untamed. Here is a country that makes everyone who comes to it stand tall and breathe deep with gratitude to God.

Many a day from the door of the cabin I had watched the rugged mountain slope receive the incomparable pomp of eve, and the cold glories of the dawn. I watched the valley gloom and gleam again with leaping sun, with dancing rain.

In the crimson end of day's declining splendor, I had often walked up the hill behind the cabin to watch the army of the stars appear. I felt the calm, majestic presence of the night bend over me with its power and might.

According to Hilaire Belloc, the mountains do two things — they make us realize how small we are, and, at the same time, they free the mind, and let it feel its greatness.

The fact is that mountains have encouraged strong religious feelings. They fill men with a sense of God's presence.

All too swiftly the hours fled by, and I had to bid a fond "farewell" to the mountains. As I took my last, long look at the beauty surrounding me, I wanted to make the promise that came from the lips of General Douglas MacArthur, "I will return." And why? Because my dreams are pinned tight to that distant mountain peak, my heart is caught high in the branches of a golden aspen back of the log cabin, my dreams are tangled in the boughs of the tallest pine.

5

A TREE LEADS TO GOD

Did you ever hear how a tree turned an atheist into a Catholic priest?

It all began one gray February afternoon along the banks of the River Charles near Boston.

The young man in our story is Father Avery Dulles, S.J., son of the late John Foster Dulles, the American Secretary of State who did so much for our country in search of peace and was known as the statesman with "Seven-League Boots."

Father Dulles wrote a little book about his conversion which he called *A Testimonial to Grace*. Thanks to the gracious permission of the publishers, Sheed & Ward, I am able to give you the fascinating story.

In 1936, Avery Dulles entered Harvard University. He had neither belief in God nor in his own soul.

The thing he did have, however, was a clear, sharp and honest mind.

One gray February afternoon, the young Dulles was in the Widener Library reading a chapter from St. Augustine's *City of God* which had been assigned as reading matter.

"On an impulse," says Dulles, "I closed the book. I was prompted to go out into the open air. It was a bleak, rainy day, rather warm for the time of the year. The slush of melting snow formed a deep mud along the banks of the River Charles which I followed down toward Boston. I enjoyed the cool rain in my face, and the melancholy of the scene.

"As I wandered aimlessly, something impelled me to look in a spirit of contemplation at a young tree. In its frail branches were young buds eagerly awaiting the spring which was at hand. While my eye rested on them, the thought came to me suddenly, with all the strength and novelty of a revelation, that these little buds followed a rule, a law of which I as yet knew nothing.

"How could it be," Avery asked himself, "that this delicate tree sprang up, grew erect, and knew when to bring forth leaves and blossoms?"

Suddenly Avery realized the truth expressed by the poet Joyce Kilmer, "Only God can make a tree."

Through the thoughtful contemplation of a tree, Avery Dulles came to realize that there is a God who rules the world. During the months that followed, Avery continued his reasoning and investigation, with the result that he became a Catholic. Today Avery Dulles is a Jesuit priest, outstanding for his brilliance and learning.

If you are as observant as Father Dulles and Joyce Kilmer, each tree will show you magic only God can do.

When you look at branches of a tree in winter, they appear dead as broomsticks. Look at them again in spring, and behold the miracles! The "sticks of wood" are pushing delicate green leaves into the sunlight.

Even more amazing, the branches in an orchard can give you juicy, fuzzy-chinned peaches, delicious apples, plump plums, golden oranges, and appetizing

Tree-shaded walk where Joyce Kilmer loved to stroll when he was a frequent guest and lecturer at Campion College. It was at Campion that Joyce Kilmer gave his final lecture before leaving for the trenches of World War I, where he gave his life for his country.

apricots. No scientist in all the world can dream up such an experiment. Not even the greatest magicians of all times, no Blackstone or Houdini, ever waved a wooden stick through the air and had it fill a bushel basket with pears or figs.

Even the broomstick in your closet may speak to you of that once distant day when it, too, was a magic rod in the hand of God and wore a handsome batch of leaves, clothed in a suit of snug-fitting bark, and whispered its secrets to the gentle south winds.

In his poem, *Spring Magic,* Father James J. Daly, S.J.,* informs us:

> I visited the woods in March;
> > Winter had done his worst to them.
> I stood beneath a windy arch,
> > Dispirited and grim.
>
> "These trees," I said, "will feel again
> > No restless flicker's friendly tap,
> Nor thrill unto the tinkling rain
> > With rising tides of sap."
>
> Then what a chorus I heard rise
> > From birches, maples, elms and planes!
> "You think we're dead: trust not your
> > > eyes —
> > Life quivers in our veins.
>
> "We're deft magicians, sir, and if
> > You urge us not to be too quick,

---

*Permission has been granted to use this poem.

We'll show you, tho' we look so stiff,
    A rather clever trick.

"We'll shake our arms thus up and down,
    To prove there's nothing in our sleeves:
Our bark's too tight a fit, you'll own,
    To hide a stack of leaves.

"There's not a green leaf here concealed:
    You're free to search the entire woods.
Go, now! Return when lawn and field
    Are wet with April floods!"

I went away; and when the skies
    With drifting veils of rain were hung
I came again. Oh, the surprise
    The wizard-trees had sprung!

Their outstretched arms were laden now
    With green new leaves of tender hue!
And whence they came, or why, or how,
    I cannot tell, can you?

"What magic, say, is it that weaves
    This miracle?" I asked each tree,
It only shook its million leaves
    And chuckled gleefully.

    There is more magic in a branch than you can shake a stick at! Do you know that the leaves on the branches build the tree mostly out of water, plus the carbon dioxide we exhale? Approximately ninety-five percent of the live weight of plants is formed from elements in air and water. Every time you exhale, you are giving leaves material with which to build trees.

This breath-building operation requires two most important things — sunlight and chlorophyll. The process of manufacturing food with energy from the sun is called photosynthesis. "Photo" is a Greek word meaning light, and "synthesis" means to put together or build.

Photosynthesis is "building with sunlight," the marvelous chemical process by which green leaves use light energy to make food. When the golden rays of the sun shake hands with the green coloring matter or pigment — chlorophyll — in a leaf, green magic is in the making. The green chlorophyll takes from the sunlight the energy it needs to change water and carbon dioxide into food.

All summer long, trees soak up the sweetness of sun, and rain, and earth to give you the tang of the tangerine, the crunchy goodness of a Winesap apple, and the walnuts for fudge.

Trees are generous. They not only give you a kitchen table, and a chair to sit on, but even supply the maple syrup to pour over the golden-brown pancakes. Every time you drink a glass of orange juice or prune juice, you are bending your elbow in a toast to your friends in green, alias the trees.

When you peel an orange, notice how cleverly the contents are divided into neat sections, which you can pry apart and eat one by one. How did the tree ever figure out such a homework assignment in long division and packaging?

The answer, of course, is that every phase of

"Operation Orange" shows God's guiding hand behind each tree. Every time you bite into an orange (or apple or pear), it is God Himself who is feeding you. Not directly, of course, but through the cooperation of our friends, the trees.

During July of 1972 I had the good fortune of coming face-to-face with the massive Sierra redwoods. Though not as tall as their coastal cousins, the Coast redwoods, the Big Trees are greater in bulk. Their age ranges up to 3,500 years or more, making them the second oldest living things on Earth, next to the bristlecone pine.

The first man to bring back news of the existence of the Big Trees was almost laughed out of camp when he tried to describe their size. Small wonder, for he himself had thought for a moment that he was ill and having hallucinations when he found himself in a grove of the giant Sierra redwoods.

The "discoverer" was Gus Dowd, a hunter hired to supply meat for crews of the Union Water Company. It was the spring of 1852 and the company was building an aqueduct to bring water to the gold diggings around Murphys.

Others had preceded Dowd to the redwoods and had even carved their names on tree trunks there, but Dowd was the first to bring back an account of what he'd seen. He had to lure his skeptical camp-mates to the forest on a ruse. When they returned and confirmed Dowd's incredible story, the Big Trees, as they became known, quickly became a big attraction.

A hotel was built there in 1854 to accommodate the growing numbers of tourists who were arriving on excursions from San Francisco and other points.

Although the visitors came to wander in awe among the giant trees that towered 250 feet or more into the blue Sierra sky, they also brought the specter of destruction.

In 1853 a team of five men pitted themselves against the tallest tree in the North Grove, seeing if they could fell this forest monarch. Their axes couldn't penetrate the tough bark, their saws were too short for the 24-foot diameter of the trunk. So they used great augers and bored parallel holes through the tree. It took them twenty-two days to topple the 302-foot tall giant.

The stump was smoothed off and a house built upon it. Later it was used for dances, as a restaurant, a newspaper office, church and theater. A saloon with a bowling alley was built on the fallen trunk of the tree. All of these structures have since been removed.

In 1854 a promoter stripped the bark off another giant Sequoia to the height of 116 feet. He shipped the bark in sections to England where it was reassembled to confound British scholars who had declared that no trees of that size could exist. The rest of the ravaged and lifeless tree still stands.

The cinnamon-red trunks of the world's most massive trees are built like lighthouses or ancient castles. Although the giant sequoias are the champion heavyweights of the plant world they are not as tall as their slender coastal cousins that reach up to 367.9 feet into the California sky.

6

PEACE PIPE AT OGLALA

The poet asks, "How many ways can I say, 'I love you'?"

So far in this book we have seen many ways in which God says to us, "I love you." His love is whispered by the wind in the treetop, and speaks to us from the heart of a rose. His love is inscribed in the fragile beauty of the orchid, emblazoned in the scarlet glory of sunset, and sculptured in granite upthrusts of mountains rising like arrows into the sky.

No wonder, then, that we read in the Book of Psalms:

> How many are your works, O Lord!
> In wisdom you have made them all.
> The Earth is full of your riches.
> You send forth your spirit, they are created;

And you renew the face of the Earth.
May the glory of the Lord last forever!

If we but look, the universe can become for us a lovely, mysterious place filled with God's presence that can lead us to a certain understanding, to abiding love, to deep happiness.

"Nothing is in the intellect," said the ancient philosopher, Aristotle, "unless it has first been in the senses." At birth our minds are absolute blanks, *tabula rasa* as the philosopher would say — blackboards with nothing on them.

If you were born blind, deaf, and without the cooperation of your five senses, you would live in a world of deathly silence, stifling blackness, and utter void. Not a single idea would ever brighten the long night of your days.

It is through the world of matter that ideas enter our head. Your eye, for example, is but a sphere of matter, a ball of flesh and water, yet this magic sphere enables you to see stars poised pale on the fringes of the Milky Way, and gathering fire in frail, pink light. You see the sun rapt in flame and fury, and you gaze upon the moon, hung like a lavaliere upon the breast of night. You look upon the face of her who is the poem of your life, the width and breadth of all that you hold dear.

Knowledge of God comes to us through our senses. When your mother whispered the word "God" His name came to you by means of sound waves, vibrating molecules of air, that moved your eardrum.

And when you read the word "God" on this page, you are actually looking at three letters from the alphabet, which, in turn, are formed by dots of ink. These ink marks on paper speak to you of Him who walks upon the wings of the wind, and clouds are His chariots.

Light rays and sound waves stimulate our senses of sight and hearing. These sense stimuli supply the raw data from which the intellect abstracts universal ideas. These show us God.

We take part in the life and love of Christ Himself, by way of creature channels — bread and oil, words and water, wine and wheat.

It is quite natural, therefore, that various objects be used as symbols of Christ Himself. The Easter candle, for example, is a symbol of Christ.

When I walked down into the catacombs beneath the city of Rome, I saw many different symbols that refer to Christ.

One of these symbols you may have seen many times — on vestments the priest wears while saying Mass. It is the letter *X*. This is the first letter of the word *Christos* in Greek.

How fascinating that a bunch of grapes, or a vine, a cup of wine, and a loaf of bread symbolize the mystery of the Eucharist, and remind us of the love of Christ — giving us Himself for our food and drink.

The action of the Mass revolves around three bits of matter — water, wine and bread.

The drops of water poured into the golden chalice may be a gift from the South Pacific or the Gulf of Mexico. A beam of sunlight sparkling over the aquamarine waters of the ocean is the magic wand releasing soft vapors and gossamer mists. High in the sky these invisible ghostly mists join hands and condense to form high-flying clouds.

Finally the raindrops parachute from the clouds to bring us the liquid of life — and to give us the sparkling drops of water in the golden chalice.

All summer long the great purple grapes drank in the beauty of sun and rain until they were bursting with goodness. As the burnished suns of late summer burned into autumn, the luscious grapes were plucked and pressed. They cascaded their sun-kissed warmth into waiting vats and, finally, into the cruet that pours liquid gold into the chalice.

The circle of white bread on the golden paten may have come from the wheat fields of Montana or Kansas. The searching roots of wheat poked their fingers down into the earth to draw forth the strength that makes bread the staff of life.

At the consecration of the Mass, these gifts of ocean, sky and land are transformed into the Body and Blood of Christ.

How fascinating it is — God, the invisible and infinite, makes use of visible and finite matter in order to come to us.

During Easter Season small cakes are baked in the form of a lamb, to remind us of Christ, who is the Lamb of God. How wonderful. A cake on our table stands as a symbol of Christ Himself.

If you would like to share an adventure into new symbols, then swing up into the saddle and gallop with me in spirit to the land of Chief Red Cloud where history wears a gun in its holster, tom-toms vibrate over sagebrush flats, and the jangle of roweled spurs make music in the land of tall blue skies.

Chief Red Cloud's country, the Pine Ridge Sioux Indian Reservation, is flung like a branding iron on the western flanks of South Dakota. The reservation is corraled on the west by the majestic, brooding Black Hills, which rise like battlements of dreamland against the distant sky.

Four miles north of the little, wind-beaten town of Pine Ridge is Holy Rosary Mission. It was the great Chief Red Cloud himself who requested the establishment of the Mission. In his honor, the main building is named Red Cloud Hall.

One of the many churches on the reservation serviced by Holy Rosary Mission is Our Lady of the Sioux some twelve miles to the west, at Oglala.

In Oglala you will find two things — Our Lady of the Sioux Church, and the Trading Post. For many, long years the Oglala Trading Post was operated by my good friend, the late John Linehan, a true westerner, with a spirit of generosity as wide and open as the prairie. His beaming smile and hearty laugh were always welcome as a benediction.

Not far from the Trading Post is Our Lady of the Sioux Church. Open the door, and walk in, and you will find yourself in a new adventure. Above the altar is a wooden crucifix — stained pale red and bearing a Christus with high cheekbones, long black braids, and the loincloth of a Sioux. Beneath the crucifix on the wall is hung a peace pipe, with eagle feather and horsehair attached to the stem. The candleholders are polished buffalo horns. The antependium or decorative cover in front of the altar is made of beaded deerskin. Instead of the Latin, *Sanctus, Sanctus, Sanctus,* or the English, *Holy, Holy, Holy,* written on it, there are the equivalent words in the Sioux language, *Wakan, Wakan, Wakan.*

Mrs. Joseph New Holy, from the Grass Creek community, tanned the antependium deerhide and did all the beadwork on it, and the tabernacle veil.

My old friend, Felix Walker, painted the lovely murals and delicate frescoes. On the wall to the left of the Gospel side of the altar is painted a tepee which glows with many and varied symbols. On the smoke flaps of the mural's tepee are depicted night and day.

On the side of the tepee you see crossed peace pipes, signifying the world of moral obligations. The buffalo signifies the source of the Sioux's supply of food, clothing and shelter. The horse shows the Indian's means of transportation.

Father Paul Barnhard Steinmetz, S.J., who is the moving force behind this new church, tells us, "This church is a constant reminder of the brotherhood of man; it is an example of how Christianity can use the best of any culture and be an important force in helping the Indian people regain pride in their heritage.

"The most important action I have taken to enter the Indian's world," continues Father Steinmetz, "and to bring him into the Christian world, is to take up his sacred peace pipe. It was named 'peace pipe' because the Indians used it to call God to witness the signing of peace treaties made with the U.S. government, just as we use the Bible in our courts to administer an oath. This is actually their prayer instrument.

"The starting point in liturgical adaptation is to go back to using the sacred pipe as an instrument of prayer. It is at the center of every traditional religious ceremony of the Sioux and all other Plains Indians. By adapting the pipe, we achieve a starting point for understanding in the Indian's mind."

At religious services, Father Paul Steinmetz takes up the sacred pipe, observing all the traditional rubrics: he fills it with tobacco, holds it in his right hand, offers it to the four directions to include the entire universe in his prayer, and concludes by touching the pipe to the ground.

Father Steinmetz tells the Sioux that their sacred pipe is a foreshadowing of Christ. Christ is the eternal and living Pipe, not made with human hands. Making the pipe a symbol of Christ does not destroy the religious meaning of their tradition, but brings it to perfection and gives it even greater power.

"This association is the most important step in adaptation that the Christian churches can take," says Father Steinmetz. "It integrates the Indian tradition into Christianity at its very core."

Father Steinmetz uses the pipe in many ceremonies: blessing homes, weddings, funerals, wakes, inaugurations of tribal officials and sun dances, as well as Christmas and Easter services.

To the objection that this may be advocating a return to paganism, Father Steinmetz replies: "No. We are following the same approach that Christ used in substituting the Mass for the Jewish Paschal meal. He used one of the great Jewish symbols, the sacred meal commemorating their deliverance from the slavery of Egypt, to explain that the New Covenant was fulfilling the Jewish Covenant, not destroying it. Christ used bread and wine as the symbols of sacrifice, symbols common to all the natural religions of the world.

"In the same way, when we make the sacred pipe, the central symbol of the Indian religion, the symbol of Christ in His office of priesthood, we are saying that Christ fulfills, and does not destroy, the Sioux religion. Take away the Indian's native religion, and you have destroyed him as a dynamic part of modern America.

"I am basing my approach to the Indian people on the personal conviction that the religious values of their tradition are still valid in their Christian faith.

"The true Indian sees the divine presence in the whole world of nature. Religion is a part of his entire life. He does not put it into a compartment as modern technological man does."

The complete soundness of Father Steinmetz's convictions is echoed by Ben Black Elk, a Sioux Indian well versed in both cultures. If ever you visited Mt. Rushmore, in South Dakota, in the summer, you no doubt saw this picturesque, full-blooded Sioux in warbonnet and beaded white doeskin.

But Ben Black Elk is more than "the most photographed Sioux in history." He is an educated man, who has lectured widely on the religion and the history of his people. As a boy he attended school at Holy Rosary Mission. Here, now, are the words of Ben Black Elk: "For many years, I was leading a double life: the life of the sacred pipe, as handed down by my people from generation to generation, and my Christian life. I lived with doubts of conscience from sun to sun, wondering if I was doing wrong as a Christian when I lectured on the sacred pipe as an Indian.

"Now, after many years, Father Paul Steinmetz has brought the two together into one life. Now I have an understanding of how the two cultures, the red and the white, can live as one. Peace is in my heart."

7

THE CIRCLE OF LOVE

If you tell me that you find yourself going in circles, I will agree with you!

Each of us, as passengers of our spaceship, planet Earth, continuously circles the sun.

In addition to the circle we describe around the sun every year, we have some "brand-new circles" that have been added as a "spin-off" of our space age.

Eugene Cernan, for example, holds the title as the only astronaut to "walk in a circle" in space completely around the Earth.

Astronauts Anders, Borman and Lovell claim the distinction of being the first men to circle the moon ten times in their Apollo spacecraft.

Despite circling satellites, orbiting moon ships, Telstars, and Intelsats spinning over our heads, the most fascinating circle in the world is still the thin band of gold slipped on the finger of a bride on her wedding day.

Look at the circle of gold that is a wedding ring. Run the tip of your finger around the inside of the ring. You don't come to a sudden stop — as you would at the end of a foot rule or yardstick. The ring circles around and around without stopping. Like the love it symbolizes, it continues forever.

St. Pius X was kind enough to leave us with an interesting account of his mother. She was a devoted woman who worked as washerwoman and school janitress that her son might study for the priesthood. On the day of his episcopal consecration, she shared his joy. Long after all the great guests had gone, they sat together, the bishop and his mother.

St. Pius toyed with the bishop's ring on his finger, showed it to his mother, teased her a bit, saying, "Mother, isn't this ring of mine wonderful? Honestly, did you ever dream that this wonder of a bishop's ring would be your boy's?"

She smiled a little, and in that smile was the whole story of her life, and his, too. "Yes," she said, "it is wonderful."

Then she held up the plain golden band on her own finger. "But, son, if it were not for this little ring," she continued, "the wonder of your ring would never have been possible."

During their ninth revolution of the moon, the Apollo 8 astronauts presented their description of our closest friend in space. According to Borman the moon is a great, vast, lonely expanse of rock.

"My thoughts are very similar," agreed Lovell. "The vast loneliness up here is awe-inspiring."

Astronaut Lovell's comment on "the vast loneliness" of the moon reminds me of the words of a song, written by my good friend, the late Father Daniel Lord, S.J.: "What's the use of moonlight if you're sad and all alone?"

The poet reminds us, "To be in Paradise alone, would be misery untold."

The ancient Greek philosopher, Aristotle, said,

"Without friends no one would choose to live, though he had all goods."

To be all alone, whether on the moon, or on Earth, would, indeed, by "misery untold."

No wonder the Bible says, "It is not good for man to be alone."

Commenting on these words of Scripture, Father John A. O'Brien reminds us that the diversity of human nature which prompts man and woman to find the compliment of their own incomplete nature in the conjugal union, the Church views as a reflection of God's will. To belittle this plan, to disparage this divinely implanted hunger, to sneer at the great endowment of sex, would be to manifest disrespect for God Himself.

Ed Doherty, famous newspaperman and author, tells us that he was fifteen years old before he knew anything of the mystery of women. Then one of his priest teachers enlightened him about them, putting the story in such words that young Ed Doherty was fired with beauty and henceforth thought of woman as God's most glorious miracle, as living poetry.

A poet may tell you that woman is a song. In a quiet moment she walks into your mind, and you remember the sound of her voice, the movement of her hand, the peace in her eyes, and — more than these — a strange, rare essence that reminds you of heaven. Woman is mystery and tenderness, strength and rapture.

Poet and sage, in song and prose, extol woman's place in daily life as well as in the history of nations. Woman is destined to be standard-bearer of refinement in taste and nobility of life-views; of faithful readiness for sacrifice and unselfish devotedness. She is created by God as an ideal.

She is destined to be a flower topping the rough and hard crag, a song, a poem, a prayer in the drab prose of life.

Hers it is to be an angel of peace in the wranglings of life. Her gentle touch soothes aching wounds, wipes away the flow of tears, and smooths out the troubled wrinkles on the worried brow.

But above all, God destined her to be the protecting angel at the hearth, the appointed guardian of moral nobility for husband, son and brother.

A great Moslem mystic of the thirteenth century, a Persian poet named Rumi, said that whoever looked on a truly beautiful woman, saw God.

In our own twentieth century Pope Paul reminds us that "woman is a special reflection of God's beauty and goodness. She inspires nobility in mankind. She is a companion of man in his loneliness."

The Pope goes on to refer to woman as "the mysterious source of human life where nature still receives the breath of God in His creation of the soul."

"The beauty of woman," said a London pastor, "is a revelation of God to man."

Father Augustine P. Hennessy, C.P., editor of *Sign* magazine, continues with this theme, and says, "Woman is obviously a kind of sacrament in creation."

Why this emphasis on the dignity of woman?

Because in some respects ours is an anti-woman world. People today are under a steady barrage of propaganda which gives a distorted attitude towards woman.

Writing in *Our Sunday Visitor,* Father Dennis J. Geaney, O.S.A., is quite explicit: "*Playboy* is reminding us that the body is something to behold and sexuality is a gift to mankind about which we should not be ashamed. But it gives a double message."

The "double message" referred to by Father Geaney is that sex is unfortunately treated as a mere commodity — as something quite apart from the person.

Almost at the same time Father Geaney's article was published, there appeared a similar article by a Catholic layman, who made practically the same comments. Neither writer took *Playboy* to task for "making manifest the beauty of the human body, which is the work of God's creation."

Rather, both writers opposed the *Playboy* attitude that cheapens sex, and makes it a mere "commodity." A woman's body becomes simply a "plaything" for the pleasure of men. When a woman loses her youth and beauty, she is tossed aside on the junk heap, to be passed by without thought or consideration, like an empty beer can, or crumpled cigarette container.

Christians should not treat other human beings in the *Playboy* manner, as disposable consumer products.

To look upon sex as merely a biological experience is to contradict the whole Christian ethic of genuine love based on honest commitment and lasting, sincere regard. Mere biological sex is psychologically devastating. Someone always seems to become the victim with feelings of having been used. This is such a brutal fact that a sex movie advertised in the amusement section of the Sunday morning newspaper had this subtitle, "People are things. Things are to be used."

True love seeks the good of another. St. Paul tells us, "Love edifies." It builds an edifice or dwelling where the other can grow and be happy. It does not make demands, it is "patient, kind, never selfish, takes no offense, and is always ready to trust, hope and endure" (1 Corinthians 13).

A man who understands the meaning of true love can say to a woman whom he loves, but who can never be his, "Because I love you, I wish you good, I want to secure for you the greatest gift and most priceless treasure — the blessing of almighty God. This blessing can be secured only through the observance of God's will, as expressed in the Commandments. My greatest tribute to you, the greatest proof of my love, will consist in my living each day according to God's will. By so doing, I am securing for you the greatest gift love can possibly secure — the blessing and good favor of God."

A young man with love-light shining in his eyes like twin stars from Paradise, if he follows this ideal of true love, will not grow raging mad as a grizzly bear if the girl of his dreams decides to marry someone else.

Since true love consists in wishing another well, the young man will rather rejoice that his dream girl has found happiness — even though she found that happiness in the arms of another.

This ideal of true love is brought out beautifully by Michael Kent in his beautiful and inspiring book, *The Mass of Brother Michel*. The hero of the story had lost his heart in the depths of a pair of dark brown eyes, shot through with flashes of fire, that sparkled in a clear young face framed in a mass of burnished curls. Into this beauty the threads of Michel's life were tightly woven, the two forming one fabric, one design.

Alas, their paths went different ways, and the girl of radiant beauty became the wife of another man. Yet, Michel, realizing that true love is based on God, said, "I shall love her till I die — yes, and through eternity, because the love I have for her is of that sort which God not only permits but enjoins upon us, and wills shall last forever. It is a love which is all joy and all peace; which desires only her good and her happiness wherever God decrees that she shall find it."

"What are men better than sheep and goats," asks the poet, "if, knowing God, they lift not hands in prayer?"

We may go on to say that the "sheep and goat" attitude some people have towards woman is simply a reflection of their outlook on life.

The nonbeliever who looks on life as a senseless form of mere animal existence flickering like an unsteady candle flame between two dark chasms of utter nothingness, can have only an animal attitude towards what he probably sees as a stupid, mixed-up thing called life, which is today, and tomorrow vanishes like a dream in the night. To the agnostic, life is without meaning, hence, it means nothing to live like an animal. For "what are men better than sheep and goats?"

For the unbeliever, all paths of glory lead but to the grave, and since the grave is the end of everything, fill the unforgiving minute with sixty seconds of mad pleasure. Hobble your brains with a pint of raw whisky, or live it up at a fashionable nightclub amid a blaring syncopation of light, heat and sound.

The sun drops to the west of Sunset Strip where rise some of Hollywood's fine shops, the posh supper clubs, some with legendary names: Ciro's, Scandia, La Rue. Now the Strip is invaded by hippies, acid-heads with long hair, sandals, and strings of beads — and psychedelic shops which carry buttons and placards proclaiming, "Happiness Is A Sugar Cube."

Pity the hippie who seeks an existence in which he is committed neither to past values nor future causes. With his focus on the present, he is determined to experience everything he can. Despairing of any hope for guidance from the past, pessimistic toward the possibility of altering the world in which he will live, he turns to himself. He is often promiscuous. His devotion to potent drugs sometimes takes on religious intensity.

The hippie is proof that a man's way of acting is determined by his attitude towards life.

The man whose world is balanced on love of God, and held steady by the gyroscope of faith, realizes that we are not doomed to vanish from the sky like sputtering Sputniks, or the burnt-out booster section of a Saturn 5 rocket leaping towards the moon.

The Christian religion is one of optimism, of hope, and of courage. At Mass the Church bids us, "Lift up your hearts."

Had God so wished, He could make each man individually. Instead, in a sweeping and splendid act of generosity, God shares His creative power with each man and woman, giving them the stupendous power of bringing future citizens into this wonderful world, and into the kingdom of heaven.

"When will men be like gods?" is a question already answered. Through the marvelous power of sex, man is already god-like. How awe-inspiring to realize that men and women have a power like unto that of the Creator Himself.

What a compliment to us to realize that the great God who balances planets in the hollow of His hand, and who lights the stars in the heavens, this kind, all-loving God wants to share His power with us.

God stands waiting for the cooperation of husband and wife to give them children to love.

Some of the most beautiful things in the world come to us through sex. "God has left us three things from Paradise," the poet reminds us, "the stars, the flowers, and the eyes of a child."

The face of a little child reading is like a deep quiet pool you find in the forest which receives in its stillness all the wonders of the wide, clean sky.

In a letter written to G. K. Chesterton, H. Belloc reminds us that if a man climbs to the stars and finds the secrets of the angels, the best and most satisfying thing he could do is to play with children.

A child's world is balanced on faith, and warmed in the peace and security of its mother's love. The luster of a child's untarnished eyes reminds us that "heaven lies about us in our infancy!"

Life is an adventure with Christ. He is our Companion and Friend. With such a comrade, such a friend, we are glad to walk to journey's end. A journey which ends with Christ taking us by the hand,

and leading us across the threshold of a new life in our home beyond the stars.

Since life is a sacred thing, and sex is the gateway to life, sex itself becomes sacred. Husband and wife are privileged to cooperate with God in the creation of a human being. By means of sex, parents become partners with God.

Parents become priests of the Most High, co-partners in the miracle and mystery of bringing into existence a being made in the image and likeness of God.

Because the tabernacles in our churches contain the source of all life, they are holy and sacred. Because the tabernacle of a woman's body contains a source of life, it, too, is sacred and holy.

Each girl's body is a living chalice containing the precious life of future children.

Around a beautiful and precious work of art men throw a cordon of protection. The famous crystal chalice of Antioch, which our Lord is said to have used at the Last Supper, is considered so precious that men have protected it by a magnificent outer cup of skillfully hammered silver of exquisite beauty and design.

Around His loving and charming daughters, God throws a cordon of protection, and says, "These are my beloved daughters, who some day may cooperate with their husbands in helping Me bring into this world future citizens of the kingdom of heaven. Acts which are beautiful, and wonderful in marriage, are intended for this state only."

Young men, hearing this call, realize that some day they may share with God the Father His very Fatherhood. Their bodies are shrines of life, and shrines are holy things. Their bodies are temples of the future, and something sacred, almost divine.

In a survey conducted by *Life* magazine, it is interesting to note that despite the so-called "new morality" and the "liberalized ideas" of some "moderns" the vast majority of Americans still stand by the ideals and aspirations of "traditional marriage."

Marriage may not always be blissful after the honeymoon is over, but it fulfills a basic human need as nothing else can. It is consoling and comforting to know that two people are happy to stand beside each other, to love, and to give of themselves freely, no matter what the changing circumstances around them.

A young couple mapping out their future are like two explorers standing before a giant mountain looming skyward from a forest of uncertainties. Alone, they would be incomplete, unhappy, and afraid of the gloom lurking in the shadows. Even a bright day in June would fail to warm their hearts when they walked alone. Their most intense joys, and sparkling happiness would appear frustrating without someone to share their moments of glory.

But together! What an upsurge of confidence and joy! They feel confident to climb the highest mountain, scale the steepest peak. They can plan and build for the future. As long as they can walk hand in hand, everything makes sense.

8

MOTHER

"When you looked into Mother's eyes, you knew, as if He had told you, why God had sent her into the world — it was to open the minds of all who looked to beautiful thoughts." With these words James M. Barrie reminds us of the glory of one's mother.

Poetry, art, music, all that can express man's sincere sentiments are eloquent of his esteem for his mother. And few are the sons and daughters who have learned to serve God unguided by a mother's hand.

St. Augustine, whose saintly mother, Monica, for seventeen long years prayed for his conversion from a life of evil, said of her, "It is to my mother that I owe all. If I am your child, O God, it is because you gave me such a mother."

These sentiments have echoed down through the

centuries, and were caught up again by Sir Thomas Lipton, "I had a good start, for I had a good mother. The best mother God ever sent to be one of His angels on earth."

Abraham Lincoln voiced almost the same sentiments, "All that I am, or hope to be, I owe to my angel mother."

Raphael's Madonnas are said to be the image of a mother's love, fixed in permanent outline forever.

A mother who is truly a mother is always a saint in the eyes of her children. To the child the mother is not a woman only; she is his mother, a unique being whom he sets apart from all others. A mother is the personification of great and unselfish love. She watches over the lives of her little ones, is happy in their joys, and suffers in their sorrows with no thought of herself.

To the mother, the child is her child, her "little one" and he will ever remain her "little one" no matter what his age, his social position, his failures or his achievements. She it is to whom one may always go for sympathy in time of trouble or sorrow, and whose joy is fullest at the success of her child.

Mother turns a house into a home, and gives it "atmosphere." Mother, in fact, "makes the family." There are times when Mother is tempted to feel that she is left all alone to "hold the fort." All day she remains in "the thick of battle" — fighting colds, wiping runny noses, patching knees scraped on sidewalks. Mother carries on a valiant defense against overwhelming mountains of soiled clothes and dirty dishes.

There are long vigils spent at the kitchen sink,

The author at an early age with his mother.

the ironing board and the mixing board — where flour, baking soda, raisins, plus a dash of cinnamon and pure magic results in the miracle of cinnamon rolls.

Mother rivals a long-distance walker with all the

miles she chalks up pushing a vacuum cleaner, dusting furniture and mopping floors.

My friend, Father Daniel Lord, said that all his life with his mother was a training. This training went on in a thousand ways. Though it was most powerful, this training was neither formal nor planned. It was simply the result of his constant companionship with his mother.

We can control and improve only those we well know. This means that the mother's part in training the child is predominant. Fathers, too, have their part. But Dad's part as breadwinner means that he is absent from home most of the day.

The destiny of every man is bound up by the ties of his very flesh and blood with the destiny of his mother. It is her destiny to fashion him so that whatever be his state of life, he will always desire to work for God.

Mother's belief in the worth and the possibilities of her child qualify her as the educator *par excellence.*

The home is the child's first classroom. Here, in an atmosphere of love and understanding, a child should be molded in body and mind into the type of citizen who will be a credit to the nation.

The home is the first laboratory for good citizenship. It is the basic unit in our society. It should be the medium for teaching ideals of conduct that will make its future citizens law-abiding, and responsible.

Most people love to revisit their childhood home. Even though it is changed, and the old familiar faces are gone, there is still a magnet pulling us to our one-time home.

The source of the perpetual attraction is that the

love of a mother and father once dwelt there, and to this shrine we return to seek renewal and the inspiration to nobler purpose.

"The most important person on earth," said Joseph Cardinal Mindszenty, "is a mother. She cannot claim the honor of having built Notre Dame Cathedral. She need not. She has built something more magnificent than any cathedral. Mothers are closer to God the Creator than any other creature. What on God's good earth is more glorious than this: to be a mother?"

"God is love," says St. John. But only the person who has experienced love knows what it is. It is through the love of those near and dear to us that we are led to God, who is Love Itself. Only through love can we draw near to God.

The greatest gift parents can give a child is the gift of love. After a quarter of a century of working with young people, I realize only too well that the child to be pitied most is the one who never received love from his parents. The most damaged personalities are those of people who were told by one or both parents, "We do not love you. We do not want you!"

What happens to the child who grows up in a home where there is no love — where there is wrangling, bitterness and even hatred?

This child cannot even believe that there is a thing called love.

When you tell him that God is Love, he does not know what you are talking about.

One of the most priceless treasures parents can give their children is their love for him and for one another.

If children grow in this atmosphere of love, if they develop in it, if they are almost "bathed" in the warmth and love of their home, they can grow into integrated human beings. They are able to be fulfilled by the love of God.

If children are the recipients of love, it is possible for them not only to respond to love, but for them to understand and give it.

Children seeing love exhibited will know what Christianity is: the acceptance in faith of the mystery of God, who is Love.

The experience of love is needed to understand that God is Love.

An old Talmudic proverb says that since God could not be everywhere, He created mothers. It is through the experience a child has with his mother that he draws his picture of the great, wide world around him. If the mother is loving, the child will consider the world is loving. If the child is not loved, it fails to learn to love.

There is no substitute for genuine love.

We conclude this chapter with a prayer from the Christophers:

> Praise to You, Father
> for the innocent eyes of children
> for sunlight and flowers and snowfalls
> for the minds of scholars who unfold
>   the truths of the universe
> for the hearts of parents
> who teach us to love.

9

THREE MAGIC WORDS

What is the most necessary and most powerful vitamin in the world?

It is a vitamin you won't find in orange juice, or cod-liver oil. It does not come in bottles or pills.

According to Dr. Miner C. Hill, a pediatrician who has cared for more than 8,000 families, the vitamin most necessary for all of us is the vitamin of love.

The vitamin of love is the greatest single gift parents can bestow upon their children. Those who were blessed with the vitamin of love when they were young will mature into well-adjusted adults, and will pass on this precious gift to their own children.

An outstanding scientist, Dr. Ashley Montagu, goes even further and refers to the awesome power of human love as the single most important force in shaping our physical, emotional and spiritual lives.

Love is the most important experience in the lives of each of us!

Love is even more important for a baby than milk! Even though a child is physically well cared for, he may, nevertheless, waste away and die.

Lack of love can kill!

Because this was not understood during the first two decades of this century, most of the babies in children's institutions never came out alive!

At a meeting of the American Pediatric Society in 1915 Dr. Henry Chapin gave a report on ten infant asylums in which, with only one exception, every child under two years of age died.

As late as 1915, some ninety percent of the children in Baltimore orphanages died within the first year of admission. Only slowly did pediatricians come to discover that the children were dying from lack of love.

Children are not the only ones who die from lack of love. According to the British Medical Journal, many widowed persons die within six months to a year following the loss of their spouses. It is thought that bereavement can aggravate a heart condition sufficiently to cause death. The sorrowing loved one dies from a broken heart!

According to the psychologist, love is not a luxury. It is a necessity. The need for love begins in infancy, and continues through life. With its first faint beating, the human heart begins its deathless cry for love and friendship.

Our heart is made for love. Love, indeed, is the life of our heart. Human love is a great and precious treasure. It is the most intense human gratification here on earth. More than anything else our hearts crave love, and love more than anything else gives delight to the heart of man.

Love is indispensable. Mother love is absolutely necessary for children's healthy and happy growth, both physical and spiritual. Love is part of personal education; through love, the self learns to grow. Love of beauty and of all lovely and wonderful things is equally vital for our growth and the realization of our possibilities. Personal love is indispensable for the full development of the individual.

Love is a positive emotion, an enlargement of life; it leads on toward greater fulfillment. It brings reverence and a sense of transcendence into our lives.

The three most exciting, thrilling and satisfying words in the world are, "I love you."

These words bring Paradise to Earth, and echo a divine refrain that returns like a haunting melody.

At the sound of these magic words heaven opens its portals. Wonder-wide eyes sparkling like twin stars with love-light from above become the gateway to Paradise. A single gaze sharp as a sword tip, or soft as candle flame, sends heat lightning quivering through your pulse, thunder pounding in your veins. One glance sets your heart drumming like pony feet on the hard, dry earth of fall.

The lover reads the eyes and studies the gestures of his beloved for guarantees of his exciting assurances. He devours her face and her image, fixing them in his mind, that he may possess them forever. His heart ticks off each moment, awaiting her return, and fills the long hours with joyous anticipation.

Her personality is a glowing fire against the blackness of time. Her voice a light bell striking melody through the long emptiness. He remembers how her hand in his sent armies with banners charging through his veins. He remembers that first breathless moment when beauty stirred a tumult in his soul that would never die.

"Down the nights, and down the days . . . down the labyrinthine ways" of his own mind, she walks, silent and serene. Like an invisible companion of childhood, she becomes more real than creatures of flesh and blood who surround him.

When love flows like a mighty river into our hearts, it bathes the world in the glow of its radiance. Love, strong and powerful as an ocean tide, sustains us in dark hours of hesitation and through dreary days dull with monotony and irksome with questioning doubts. Love makes each moment a precious memory, each hour a lifetime, each day a glittering treasure.

A man in love walks upon the wings of the wind, and the clouds are his chariots. A name shouts through his mind, and echoes a thousand memories of sheer joy. A face is framed in his thoughts that radiates smiles of happiness and excitement. Every fiber of his being vibrates with joy at being one in spirit with her who is life itself, and joy and happiness. His whole existence circles around her who is his sun, and moon, and the center of his universe.

When the sun surrenders to the starlight and the night is drawn out like soft silver music, the trembling leaves embrace the breeze, the man in love gives voice to a prayer his lonely heart has set to music. His soul kneels as he whispers that his loved one is a dream concerto played on the strings of his heart. Like a golden harp gently caressed, the silver music enters his heart to stay there forever.

The poet tells us:

> Love is a star from heaven, that points the way
> And leads us to its home, a little spot
> In earth's dry desert, where the soul may rest,
> A grain of gold in the dull sands of life,
> A foretaste of Elysium.

Like a morning-glory entwining a trellis, the memory of a loved one weaves itself into the very pattern of one's life until two hearts become one.

The man into whose heart beauty looks with calm, sweet eyes finds memory dancing like a compass. From the first flush of dawn to the crimson end of day's declining splendor, a name echoes in his heart, making him vibrate with joy, and his pulse beat high with expectation.

As night approaches on soft and beautiful feet to cloak the world in a mantle of mystery and magic, his thoughts leap to the saddle and race with the wind.

The midnight hears the cry of his desire. And when the mystic moon ascends the pathway to the stars, distant lovers look upon its magic glow, and in the golden warmth of its embrace feel they are united by this messenger from space.

When the miracle that is love bursts like a

sunrise over the horizon of life, the world is bathed in the magic of its radiance.

How strange is love. It spreads beyond the distant prairie, leaps above the towering Rocky Mountains, soars into the wide, blue yonder, then blends and never ends in all of space. Love cannot be held within the boundaries of a chart, and yet, your loved one holds it in her heart!

Love flows like a river through the center of life. It is a river with many branches. In places it is wide and quiet, like a pool. Elsewhere it runs wind-driven and fierce, tearing at its banks, sweeping trees along.

It flows in an old man with slow fingers tying a child's shoelace, and in a young woman filled with the heavy joy of owning, and being owned. Pools and rapids, deeps and shoals, calm and flood — all these make the river of love.

"My eyes look down in your lovely face," a popular song reminds us, "and I hold the world in my embrace. Heaven and earth are you to me."

The two greatest joys in life are to love, and to know that one is loved.

Love springs from the heart's abundance, and the heart's need. It is an ancient charm to push the world away, to make the universe sparkling with light. It is a magic wrought by two, a secret language old as human loneliness. It is a sigh, a dream, a yearning, a surrender, captured in a sacrament.

In his autobiography Lord Russell gives us three reasons why love is the most precious of all gifts. First, it is love that brings ecstasy so great it is worth sacrificing all the rest of life for a few precious hours of this joy.

Next, it is love that relieves that terrible loneliness in which one feels shivering alone on the cold rim of space.

Finally, in the union of love we have a mystic miniature of a vision of what heaven will be like, when we will be united to our loved ones in a union of joy and happiness that will last for always.

Without love, life would be unbearable. The man whose heart is parched with loneliness knows the terrible ache and longing, the fierce want, the desperate yearning, the unsatisfied craving that turns his days into a bleak desert of shifting, burning sands. Loneliness can scorch the heart with agony, deep, terrible, overwhelming.

Like the blackness of a wind-tossed night, loneliness can torture the spirit of man. The heart utters its deathless cry for love and friendship, and in return catches only a mocking echo hurried away by wild winds. No wonder Christian Rossetti speaks of "the black death of living alone."

The man into whose life love has once walked can never be alone. Charles H. Daniels at the age of ninety-one wrote the following poem in memory of his wife, with whom he shared his life for fifty-five years:

> The memory of someone dear is like a thing of gold
> That never rusts or dulls, nor grows the least bit old.
> 'Tis like a bit of bright sunshine that fills an empty room,
> Or like a lovely flower that never fails to bloom.

> It offers consolation in the face of strife and stress,
> And adds a certain beauty to each dream of happiness.
> The memory of some dear one, however long apart,
> Is like a soothing melody that lingers in the heart.
> Or like a perfect rainbow that lingers in the sky —
> The portrait of a past that can never die!

The late Cardinal Cushing of Boston said: "I believe that to be able to remember the gift of love is the greatest gift any man shall have received in his life — because from the gift of love and the good memory of love, a man can become the whole person he was meant to become in the sight of God."

A man in love feasts his hunger on the face and figure of his loved one. To the end of his days he will carry this image as he has fixed it in his mind and heart.

The memory of an absent loved one may well be more welcome and real than the reality of others who surround us. A precious memory that shines in the fabric of our past like a thread of pure gold in a tapestry may mean the difference between hope and despair, between strength for another day, and the collapse of all meaning.

A lovely memory can nourish otherwise desolate lives. When we remember, we confer the present upon a loved one, and give the loved one further life in our own life.

We are fed and nourished by the union of two lives that intersect and mingle in memory. In truth, the memory of a loved one becomes part of us. A man in love does not forget. The one who is loved is not forgotten.

Concerning those who live without memories, Father Anthony T. Padovano says, "They have met no one they wished to abide with forever."

During the war years a wife wrote to her husband: "Constantly you are in my mind. Every morning begins with thoughts of you, and the last thought I have before sleep at night is you. Though an ocean separates us, you are beside me always. Sometimes you seem so close, I can almost feel your touch.

"The ring on my finger — I can't explain what a wonderful feeling it is to be wearing it, and knowing that I'm your wife forever. It serves as a reminder every time trouble is near that you are at my side to help, and when I'm having a rationed bit of happiness, you share it too.

"You know that in spirit, I'm always at your side with all the love there is to give.

"I'd love to be with you every breath you breathe. I feel such a marvelous feeling of warmth and contentment inside me when I think of you. Every second, you travel beside me."

Did you ever leave a concert while the melody kept echoing through your memory? So it is when you must leave the presence of a loved one, her presence lingers like an afterglow. Indeed, she cannot wholly leave, but her well-remembered face remains like music in your heart.

Some days are so dull and dreary, so filled with

worry and pain and such desolation that only two things seem to afford any consolation — the memory of the wonderful times we have enjoyed with our loved ones — and the assurance from God that on some future day in our home beyond the stars, we shall be united to those we love in a union of joy that will last for eternity.

Memory and hope are the wings that lift us above the dull sands of time and enable us to soar into the wide blue sky of God's wonderful tomorrow.

"Somewhere over the rainbow, bluebirds sing, and dreams that you dare to dream really do come true." So sang Dorothy, the little Kansas farm girl in the motion picture, *The Wizard of Oz*. In a certain sense, this song could be adopted for the Christian's theme song — for, in truth, over the rainbow of this life gleams God's glorious kingdom, our home of joy and happiness without end.

Perhaps someone may say that in the absence of loved ones the memory of what has been becomes physical pain, a mockery, an illusion: to feel one so close that you have but to extend a hand to touch him, and doing so, to find only an absence; to hear him speak, and listening, to find only silence. Is this not a mere echo, a tormenting dream? Especially when death robs us of loved ones?

If we were mere creatures of flesh and clay, destined like the grass of the field to bloom and wither away, we would find the memory of departed ones a tormenting thing — reminding us of rich joys we once had, but will never have again.

The Christian realizes that the joys and satisfactions of this life are but dim reflections of the unending joys to come, when God shall wipe away all tears from our eyes. Not even death can shatter the bond of true love.

Of all the wonderful gifts that God has given us, memory is most unique. It enables a loved one to stay alive in our hearts forever. And it is often the remembered moments of love that keep us going when it seems we have reached the limits of our endurance.

The sky is never so blue and the meadow lark never sings so sweetly as when we are overflowing with love.

A man in love can say to the queen of his heart, "This is a lovelier world because of you. You fill my days with rare delight. You are the thrill of springtime, and my wondrous wishing star.

"The songs I hear in my heart echo your gift of love. Each time we meet, a bright, gay music in me sings. My heart sprouts vibrant, flaming wings. You walk in and the song begins. When you are near to me, you are my symphony. My heart beats in rhythm to the song that is you."

According to Franz Weyergan, "If you have not known the temptation to see in one beloved face the whole glory of God, you have not known love."

Love lights fuses in your veins. It ignites skyrockets that cascade showers of golden sparks. It unleashes Roman candles lancing the darkness of the night.

In his masterful work, *A Companion To The Summa,* Father Walter Farrell, O.P., states that a loved one is never out of our minds. In fact, our minds become like a home where our loved one moves about with complete familiarity, leaving an impress on every thought, every image, every memory.

This fact is expressed in a song made popular by Perry Como: "Who knows how many times I pause in every day to think of you? As often as the sun sails out upon the silent sea. And if you wonder why it is I only think of you, well it's because I'd like to be as close to you as you've become to me."

Harold Blake Walker informs us that if we look for God only in some shattering mystical experience, we are likely to miss Him in the warmth of caring human relationships wherein He is most surely to be found. Christ repeatedly emphasized that the love of God and the love we bear for others are two sides of a single coin. We can't have one without the other.

This statement of Dr. Walker is exemplified in the experience of Father Ellwood Kieser, the talented priest who is responsible for the TV series, *Insight*.

Speaking of his college life, before he entered the seminary, Father Kieser says that early in his sophomore year he met Clair, who filled his next three years with all the joy and pain of young love.

Ellwood Kieser told Clair that he was not only loving her, but he was also loving God through her. And this not in an abstract way, but as a matter of experience.

As the years passed, Ellwood Kieser grew in the conviction that God was calling him to the priesthood, and so, on a bright Sunday afternoon in August 1950, he entered the Novitiate of the Paulist Fathers.

Following his ordination, Father Kieser worked at the UCLA Medical Center and taught at Marymount College. The television series, *Insight,* grew out of the adult educational program Father Kieser had started for adult theological education.

During the Second Vatican Council, Father Kieser was sent to Rome to do a weekly report to the American people on the happenings at the Council.

One of the exciting things about the Council for Father Kieser was a deeply moving personal experience. He had previously accepted the theory that love is the ultimate human value, and that the human is permeated with the divine. Our point of contact with the divine is the human, and to embrace the one is to embrace the other. Now the words of St. John became a glowing reality, "He who abides in love abides in God and God in him."

"I love many people," says Father Kieser, "and many people love me. I find these relationships a real experience of God. I encounter God in the one I love. I feel Him in the electricity that sings between us. I know Him in that mysterious fashion which takes place when two souls touch."

One of the most talked-of poets of our twentieth century is William Everson. He says that it was the intense love for his wife that brought him into the Church. Indeed, he goes on to say that in his life the love of God has been so intimately bound up with the love of his wife that in truth a woman led him to God.

According to Vincent Van Gogh the best way to love God is to love someone with a lofty and serious intimate sympathy, with strength and intelligence.

"One begins his communion with God," remarks Father Padovano, "when he becomes alive to human warmth and human love."

Today we are told that one of the most important things in religion is an understanding of love. If a man does not know how to love, how can he know much about the God who is Love?

Since all love comes from God, man becomes a lover of God when he enters into the experience of true love.

All of us hunger for sharing life with others. This opens to us as nothing else does the sharing of life with God Himself.

Through the love of those near and dear to us we are led to God, who is Love Itself.

It is not poetic exaggeration to say that one of the greatest things your loved one does for you is to give you a sample of the joys of heaven to come, a foretaste of heaven itself.

How wonderful it all is. Besides bestowing upon you the privilege of being loved, your loved one is helping you to come to an understanding of what God is in Himself, and is thereby leading you to the source of all beauty and love.

How consoling to realize that the love you have experienced will blend and fuse into a union of unbounded joy in heaven above.

10

THE LANGUAGE OF LOVE

We may consider our skin as love's epidermis!

Through the sense of touch love speaks a silent, but most persuasive language.

For proof consider that as late as the second decade of our enlightened twentieth century the death rate of infants under one year of age in various fondling institutions throughout the United States was nearly 100 percent — and this despite the sterilized environment of the babies, the best in hygienic conditions, and careful medical attention.

In the late '20s, some hospital pediatricians began to introduce T.L.C. (Tender Loving Care). Every baby had to be picked up, caressed, hugged, cuddled and embraced several times a day.

The results were dynamic. Following the "mothering" approach in the pediatric wards of the Bellevue Hospital in New York, the mortality rates for babies under one year dropped to less than ten percent.

The results proved that what a child needs to prosper is something more than food. A child needs love. *It is through the sense of touch that love is first communicated to us.*

Hugs, kisses, embraces, coddling, stroking — all these speak silently but powerfully of concern, tenderness, response and awareness.

In his superb book, *Touching, The Human Significance of the Skin,* Dr. Ashley Montagu informs us that if a child is to live, the messages he receives through his skin must be security-giving and assuring. A failure of adequate cutaneous stimulation for an infant is a failure in communication. The child feels it is not loved.

Dr. Montagu would have us keep in mind that it is not words so much as acts communicating affection that children, and, indeed, adults, require.

Art Linkletter tells us that when he visits orphanages he finds children so straightforward about their need for love as shown through contact that they want to touch you.

"They hang on your legs, your arms, your fingers," says Art Linkletter. "They need love so desperately. Sometimes, I just sit and hold a child."

Art Linkletter is not alone in his experiences. According to *Newsweek* magazine a group of grandmothers has been organized in Exeter, Rhode Island, to visit the Ladd School for retarded youngsters. The grandmothers bring these unfortunate children the thing they need most — love.

The grandmothers do more than give words of greetings to the children assigned to them. They hug them, kiss them, or just hold them in their arms, so that the children will know how genuinely they are loved.

The language of touch is one that is spoken everywhere, no matter what the conditions or social status of the people. In fact, at times, touch may be the only language that is understood.

In his fascinating article in the *National Geographic* magazine for August 1972, Kenneth MacLeish tells of his incredible trip to the Stone-Age cavemen of Mindanao, a tribe of people in the Philippines who live much as our ancestors did thousands of years ago.

It was the first expedition to penetrate the moun-

Tenderness, warmth, love and affection are relayed by the touch of the hand. —*Courtesy Blue Cloud Abbey*

tainous, forest-armored wilderness that has hidden the Tasadays from the world. When the men from the twentieth century came face-to-face with the men of the Stone Age, MacLeish and his men paused to give the Tasadays a chance to look at the visitors from the modern world.

Then an old man, naked except for a loincloth, came forward and embraced MacLeish. "We remained close," said Kenneth MacLeish, "bridging the immense cultural gap between us through physical contact, to show that there was no human gap at all."

The children who were sitting on the ledges saw and responded.

To understand the language of touch, watch a little boy who has been given his first, long-desired puppy. The boy shows his love for the puppy by petting it, stroking its fur, and by placing its small warm body against his face.

Imagine telling the little boy not to touch his puppy. You might as well take the puppy away from the boy completely. It is through the sense of touch that the youngster relays to the puppy his love, and the puppy in turn seeks the security and warmth of the boy's loving hand.

According to a poet, even though you travel the whole wide world over, from the leaping river of the Yellowstone to the Great Buddha of Kamakura, there is nothing so satisfying as the golden moment when your loved one reaches out to hold your hand in hers.

When beauty stands looking into your heart with calm, clear eyes, and the strings of your heart shimmer with matchless sounds, love often finds itself with nothing to say.

Love is too deep and mysterious to attempt to phrase it in mere sentences. Words are too small for the long thoughts of love.

Love often finds itself with no language except silence. When love is trying to say that which cannot be said, it becomes stammering, trembling, tongue-tied, hesitant.

Love that is so bold stops on the edge of speech, after stumbling, and can only say, "I love you."

Beyond that, all words are spent. You cannot convey love by speech. You touch it somehow by silence. In silence heart meets heart. It may happen that love has silenced you sometimes, because love has lifted you into higher realms when you are in the presence of the one you love.

"Somehow, by holding hands," says Maureen Daly in her book, *Seventeenth Summer,* "you can carry on a conversation without talking."

"Your hands in mine," says Louis Untermeyer, "sent armies with banners charging through my veins."

According to the lines from popular songs, "I hear music when I touch your hand, a beautiful melody from some enchanted land. Then slowly my fingertips find the thrill of your fingers in mine. . . ."

"Fantastic things happen when I'm in your arms. The stars desert the skies, and rush to nestle in your eyes. It's magic. . . ."

"When we walk hand in hand the world becomes our wonderland. The magic is my love for you. . . ."

Dr. Joseph W. Bird, a clinical psychologist and

psychotherapist, who has written for many publications, reminds us that no one has ever adequately explained the happiness we experience in physical contact with another. A baby stops crying when picked up by its mother. A sick child begs to have its forehead stroked. Lovers lose themselves in dreams as they hold hands. But what it is that gives us happiness and expresses love in touching, and being touched, is a mystery — a very delightful mystery, however.

No wonder Theodore Roosevelt said of his beautiful wife, Alice, "When we are alone, I cannot bear her a minute out of my arms."

According to Dr. Bird, caresses communicate tenderness, warmth, consideration and affection, and thus they become expressions of love many times over.

An inspired writer, whose name is unknown, points out for us: "If one were to put in a book all the most beautiful moments the world has ever known, he would have to mention, along with God's act of creation, or the instant of a baby's birth, the moment when two people in love kiss. For a kiss is a sacred thing — a sign of two hearts that see and love the good in each other ... and yet look beyond each other to the Goodness that brought them together."

Here, indeed, according to a poet, is a jewel to cherish forever in memory's treasure chest — that first breathless kiss like the sting of rain when beauty stirred a tumult in your heart that would never die.

"I love you so much, I could eat you!"

When a young man with love-light shining in his eyes says this to the girl of his dreams, it does not mean that he is considering turning to cannibalism.

Nor does it mean that he is so overcome by the idea that girls are made of "sugar and spice and everything nice" that he considers the object of his affection to be a cinnamon bun.

When Jack says to Debra, "I love you so much, I could eat you," he is simply expressing the fact that love craves for union, even assimilation with the one it loves.

Watch Francine hug the new doll she got for Christmas. Go down to the airport and watch Mother and Dad embrace Karen upon her return from college. Like a magnet, love is attracted by, and wishes to be united to the object of its affections.

Sometimes the desire to be united with a loved one becomes a dull ache and pain. In his beautiful book, *The Mass of Brother Michel,* Michael Kent tells us how the desire for an absent loved one can become "a fierce want and hunger, a craving unsatisfied, an emptiness, and longing."

Maureen Day describes the exquisite torture during a meal of being seated at a dinner table near someone you love — near enough to see, but not near enough to hold hands. At first you eat up your loved one by long-distance eyesight, then, there is the gnawing yearning to reach out until your fingertips entwine. Alas, a stubborn table intervenes, and all you can do is to depend upon a fleeting glance to say so many lovely things.

In an attempt to secure a unity of being, we read of romantic lovers who slit their blood vessels in their wrists and placed them together so that their blood stream would intermingle, thus making them a part of each other, both sharing, as it were, one and the same life.

St. Augustine wrote of his friend, "I thought of his soul and my soul as one in two bodies."

Archbishop Sheen reminds us, "In true married love it is not so much that two hearts walk side by side through life. Rather two hearts become one heart."

So far we have made mention of the young man with love-light in his eyes, who said, "I love you so much, I could eat you." We made mention of romantic lovers who wanted even their blood streams to mingle so that they would both share the same life.

Did you ever stop to realize that something very close to this happens in Holy Communion? Christ loves us so much He unites Himself to us in the closest way possible. At the Consecration of the Mass we hear again His words, "Take this all of you, and eat it: this is My body."

And then, "Take this all of you, and drink from it. This is the cup of My blood."

Father Thomas H. Moore, S.J., would have us keep in mind that Christ gave us His own sacred body. And the bond which weds man and wife is the sacramental sign of that greater union which wedded the Son of God to the sons of men.

St. Paul compares the union of man and wife in marriage to the union between Christ and His Church.

Commenting on these words of St. Paul, Bishop Joseph Holzner says that the relationship between Christ and the Church cannot be more beautifully expressed than by the figure of marriage, and marriage could not have been more ennobled than by this mystical reference.

Msgr. John C. Knott tells us: "The physical attraction between man and wife leading to a desire for union, important as it is in itself, is but a reflection of and a means to achieve the deeper desire for union with another person. It is a reflection of and a means to achieve man's basic and ultimate desire to be one with God!"

The loss of ego boundaries, the transcendent sense of total union which true love brings reminds us again of still another expression. We speak of someone being "on fire with love."

Why this expression?

Because fire not only strives for union with what it embraces, but seeks to transform whatever it embraces into itself. Love does likewise.

With this radiant truth burning in his mind, St. Peter Canisius wrote, "It is not enough that Christ should for our sake be made obedient unto death, even the death of the Cross. He desired further to be, in a manner of speaking, consumed utterly by us, and blended intimately with us. He must form, so to say, one with us, and that not by faith only, but by truly making us His body.

"As it happens to a coal to be changed and totally converted into fire, so by a worthy reception of the Eucharist, we become changed in a wonderful manner into Christ, are made partakers of His divine nature, and grow somehow to be the very blood-brother of Him, our Head, for so great is the power of this divine Food that whosoever eats of it worthily is not only joined to Christ by a spiritual relationship, but even made one with Him by a certain natural and most intimate incorporation."

How marvelous! This union between Christ and His people is similar — according to St. Paul — to the union of man and wife in marriage.

St. John phrases the truth in this sentence: "God is Love, and he who abides in Love abides in God and God in him."

"Real love everywhere," says Father Eugene Kennedy, "is a share in the life of God, the presence of the Spirit of Love that is neither lessened nor divided no matter how many persons share in it."

There is no delight more magical than the surprise of being loved.

The greatest gift we can receive is that of love. The best gift we can give is love.

When we experience true love, we experience God, for God is Love.

11

A GIRL LEADS TO GOD

Did you ever hear the story of how a little girl led a world-famous Communist to God?

It all began in an apartment on St. Paul Street in Baltimore. The beautiful, little daughter of former Communist Whittaker Chambers was in her high chair eating breakfast.

According to Mr. Chambers, his little girl was the most miraculous thing that had ever happened in his life. He liked to watch her eat, even when she smeared porridge on her face, and dropped it meditatively on the floor.

"My eye came to rest on the delicate convolutions of her ear," said Whittaker Chambers. "The thought passed through my mind: No, those ears were not created by any chance coming together of atoms in nature (the Communist view). They could have been created only by immense design. The thought was involuntary and unwanted. I crowded it out of my mind. But I never wholly forgot it or the occasion.

"I had to crowd it out of my mind. If I had completed it, I should have had to say: 'Design presupposes God.' "

Try as he might, Whittaker Chambers found that he could not shut the thought from his mind. At last, he had to admit to the world that "design does, indeed, presuppose God." The "miracle" that was his little girl led him to God.

A little girl has been defined as a brief mysterious creature lovely as a day in June, and running bare-kneed through the clover. She flings her arms to the deep blue heavens, and matches the skylark with a song chased by the leap of her heart. She has the face of a Botticelli angel that glows with elfin innocence — a combination of daybreak openness and midnight mystery.

She is sweeter than the violets of spring, and a deeper mystery by far than the universe of pulsing stars. She startles us with exquisite surprise with flashes of what heaven itself must be.

Her friends are the tall sky, and the great trees, the sun that smiles and marches to the sea. Her world sparkles with the crystal of dewdrops, the shimmer of moonbeams, and dazzling fountains catching freshly minted sunlight to toss like gold coins amid the silver spray.

Her laughter is delightful as a carillon of bells. And when she greets you, your spirit sprouts tiny, flaming wings, and a glad, strange music in you sings.

To hold her hand in yours is to know a miracle divine.

The poet, Naomi Parks, tells us, "The tender kiss of a little child is a jewel in a setting of love."

The ancient philosopher Plato knew that "in facing beauty, wings grow in our souls." St. Augustine goes still further and informs us that by beauty man is borne up to God.

We want God to reveal Himself, and one way God does it is through beauty.

The beauty of a child reflects the beauty of God. The more man sees this beauty, the closer he will be to seeing God who is Beauty Itself.

To experience and reflect on the goodness of a child is a compliment to God.

A child's world is balanced on faith, and warmed in the peace and security of its parents' love. The luster of a child's untarnished eyes reminds us that "heaven lies about us in our infancy!"

Sandra Hochman tells us: "Before my child was born, I could not believe the miracle. Now that she is here, I cannot believe the miracle."

Parents thrill to the music of a child's laughter, and to the infinite trust of a child's hand.

In a letter written to G. K. Chesterton, H. Belloc remarked that if a man had climbed to the stars, and found the secrets of the angels, the best and most useful thing he could do would be to come back to earth and romp with children.

"I feel sorry for all people," says Sandra Hochman, "who do not have access to children."

And no wonder, for children seem to have caught the words of Albert Einstein, "The important thing is not to stop questioning . . . never lose a holy curiosity."

For children even ordinary things take on a magical quality. Snowflakes and roses are miracles. The child walks with his senses wide open, and, like the poet, finds everything ordinary, extraordinary.

Parents are reassured by the curiosity of their new baby. "He notices," they brag as soon as his eyes in curiosity appear to follow their movements or a swinging toy.

After a quarter of a century of teaching young people, the hardest thing I find is to deal with people who have no interests. The difference between a person who seems totally alive and one completely inert is the extent and variety of their curiosity.

According to my long-time friend, Dan Lord, curiosity not only underlies all discovery and leads to all invention, but it is much more than that. It is a promise of eternal happiness. God gave us this appetite, and He means to satisfy it.

God does not intend for us to die with only the tiniest point in the inexhaustible universe tentatively explored. Even the best of us, according to Thomas Alva Edison, know only one millionth of one percent about anything, hence, God will have to give us the unlimited opportunity of all eternity to satisfy it.

Did you ever walk through a library and realized, with a sense of utter futility, the impossibility of recapturing even a small section of the past recorded there?

How thrilling it would be to have heard Socrates talk! To have been at the Globe theater on the opening night of Hamlet! To have heard Homer as he strummed his lyre! To have seen the unveiling of the bas-reliefs of the Acropolis! To have watched Michelangelo at work!

We shall take our curiosity with us into eternity, like an inexhaustible reservoir that we have never been able to fill. And then we shall be faced with the glorious paradox, the exciting contradiction: our curiosity will range out into infinity, always satisfied, and always hungry.

We never grow weary of a really beautiful painting or a lovely face. In heaven we shall be face-to-face with God Himself, who is Beauty Itself.

Upon his return from the moon, Astronaut Neil A. Armstrong said, "Mystery creates wonder and wonder is the basis for man's desire to understand."

Those who have preserved their curiosity will agree with Walt Whitman:

> Why, who makes much of a miracle?
> As for me, I know of nothing else but miracle.
> Whether I walk the streets of Manhattan
> Or talk by day with any one I love.
> . . . one and all are miracles.

We should do like children and make every day an adventure! We should look at each day as though it were ours to enjoy for the first time. We should live expectantly, and watch for the turns in the road that suddenly open new vistas of beauty before us.

Nothing will sustain us more powerfully than the power to recognize in our humdrum routine, the true poetry of life — the miracle of the commonplace.

There are miracles to be found on every hand, if only we will permit ourselves to behold them in that silent and innocent wonder which is reverence's other name.

To be young at heart is the thing that counts. Children live in a love for the beauty that is in the world, in the lofty mountains, the boundless sea, the azure sky, and in the lovely faces of those they cherish.

We should tune ourselves into the world's orchestra of living sound, the warm south wind whispering through the grain, a skylark exploding with ecstatic notes as dawn dynamites the horizon, the patter of rain on leaves, and the joyous lilt of children's laughter.

The greatest miracle of all is love. It brings inner meaning to our tenderest moments, and sustains us in difficulties. G. K. Chesterton reminds us:

> Sunlight in a child's hair
> Is like the kiss of Christ upon all children.
> I blessed the child; and hoped the blessing
>   would go with him;
> And never leave him;
> And turn first into a toy, and then into a
>   game,
> And then into a friend,
> And as he grew up, into friends,
> And then into a woman.

Some girls blossoming into womanhood imagine that they will be lovely and attractive only if they are sculptured like a Greek statue. A statue may, indeed, have lovely proportions, but marble is unresponsive as stone, and utterly lacking in affection. Physical perfection alone does not make a girl gracious and charming. A beautiful girl, in fact, may be much like an iceberg, cool to look at, but frigid and remote as the Arctic, with a personality frozen in self-isolation.

Famed designer of high-fashion clothes for women, Emilio Pucci reminds us that when woman is reduced to a statue, that is all she is.

A quite ordinary-looking girl may have a beauty of character, a sparkle of personality, a warmth of friendship, and a glow of love that make her more lovely and charming than the mascara-lidded creature with a coiffure so elaborate she has to have two others hovering around her like Nubian slaves to catch the wisps of hair and shore up the coils that have broken loose.

According to Emilio Pucci a woman's greatest qualities are her femininity, gracefulness and mystery.

Young women should keep in mind the words of the man who has painted America's most glamorous women. Rene Bouche is one of the most sought-after portraitists of American and international society. He is convinced that the most appealing quality a man finds in a woman is elegance. This elegance has nothing to do with class or money. It is found among all socioeconomic groups. It is even independent of age.

Elegance is a certain way of thinking and of looking at the world. Because elegance comes primarily from within, it is part of one's character and personality.

The elegant woman keeps her eyes open and her mind attuned to everything about her. She is continually learning, observing, studying, seeking new harmonies and proportions in the life around her.

Personality, like electricity, defies definition. Nobody knows what electricity really is, but we do know what it does for us in our daily lives. So it is with personality. We can feel it, and we can recognize its manifestations.

Personality is not a specific quality. Enthusiasm, loyalty, honesty, poise, tact, courtesy, ambition, and industry — all these are tied in with expressions of personality.

In the central places of every heart there's a recording chamber; so long as it receives messages of beauty, hope, cheer and courage, that's how long you are young. When the wires are all down and your heart is covered with the snow of pessimism and the ice of cynicism, then, and then only, are you grown old.

Some thirty years ago, when I was chaplain at St. John's Hospital in St. Louis, I witnessed the final, inspiring chapter in the life of a girl whose deep faith led her parents and all who knew her ever closer to God.

Billie was an only daughter. Her one older brother had given his life for his country in World War II. Billie was the very poem of her parents' life. Around her their lives revolved, as do the planets around the sun. She was the essence of all that they held dear, and the dream of all their future held of peace and joy.

Her mere presence clothed an event or a moment

with an iridescence that sparkled like a diamond fresh from the gem cutters of Amsterdam. Her eyes, soft as candle smoke and lambent as twilight, had the look of the forest at dusk, when the trees are all in shadow and filled with mysterious colors that have no name. Though wires of pain pulled and jerked her delicate body almost constantly, she managed a smile warm and enchanting as springtime.

Billie's parents spent as much time as they could alongside the bed of suffering and pain that had been Billie's prison and martyrdom for many long torture-filled weeks that alternated between quivering hope, and utter helplessness.

From them I learned a tremendous lesson that overpowered me with its impact. In times of pain and suffering — be it physical or mental — we are often helpless to aid those we love. There is *nothing we can do!*

We would so like to have a magic wand, and with a single encircling gesture, remove all pain and suffering from the lives of our loved ones.

Alas, there are far too many times when we do or say *absolutely nothing* to take away the pain that cuts deep and fierce as a razor. We are helpless to take away the emptiness and longing that torture both mind and heart.

During such agonizing times, we can *only be* with those we love. If we cannot be with our loved ones in person, we can be with them in spirit. Even though we may be separated by many long horizons, we can leap the distance in one flash of thought chased by the desire of our heart, and be with those we love in spirit and keep them in our prayers.

The main thing that impressed all who came to visit Billie and her parents was their spirit of faith. Both Billie and her parents were fully aware of the fact that the days of her life were numbered and fast slipping away. This fact did not disturb nor dismay them, rather, they looked forward to the coming event with confidence, knowing that Billie was going forth to place her hands into the hands of Christ, and that one day in the future there would be a family reunion of joy and happiness in heaven.

Billie's attitude reflected that of the nineteen-year-old Polish boy, St. Stanislaus Kostka. When informed that he would not recover from a fatal sickness, and that death was fast approaching, the boy was not in the least saddened. Rather his face glowed with calmness and happiness. Echoing the words of the Psalmist, he exclaimed: "I rejoice at the things that are told unto me. We shall go into the house of the Lord."

It was an interesting coincidence to note that at the time Billie was in St. John's Hospital in St. Louis, an attractive blond boy, Donald Redfearn, was dying from bone cancer in an Illinois hospital just across the Mississippi River. The newspapers carried the account of his final days. When visitors asked him whether or not he was saddened by the thought of death, Donald looked up from his hospital bed, and replied, "When I think of dying and going to heaven to see God, I can hardly wait."

What inspiration these young people give us!

In the early ages of the Church the day on which a person died was considered to be his "birthday" — his "birthday" into joy and glory.

It was in this spirit that Billie's parents took the death of their lovely daughter. They had not lost a daughter, but, rather, gained a saint of their own in heaven. They knew that the girl they loved would be theirs forever. Her love for them would shine like a silver star. The words of St. Paul echoed in their memory, "We shall be with the Lord forever. Tell one another this for your consolation."

With these glorious words from St. Paul ringing in his ears, the Christian realizes that death is not the end of life, even for a second. Death is merely the division point between two lives. Death is not a wall that rises to block all human progress. Death is merely a passport that admits you to joy forever.

Death to the Christian is a rebirth, a new and wonderful life. In the Preface of the Mass on the day of burial we are reminded that "life is changed, not taken away; and though the abode of this earthly habitation is destroyed, an everlasting home is prepared in heaven."

Death is a change from life to larger life. It is a birthday. The beginning of joy forever.

Naturally we feel the pain of separation from loved ones, but our faith hallows and tempers this sorrow. The words of St. Paul are words of consolation. They mean that all those you love will be yours for always. If they have departed this life before you, then know they will be waiting to welcome you into the joy of the Lord, into the kingdom of heaven, where God will wipe away all tears, and death will be no more.

Thanks to the doctrine of the communion of saints, we know we may keep in contact with our dear ones in heaven through the wonderful privilege of talking to them in prayer. This is consolation, indeed. You need never "feel alone with the beating of your heart" for just as surely as your veins pulse with life, your loved ones are by your side to talk to, and listen to your heartaches and sorrows, joys and plans.

Companionship with our dear departed ones can afford us deep joy and consolation. That it is an unseen presence does not make it less valuable. And their help is nonetheless powerful for being unseen by physical eyes.

So strong was the faith of Billie's parents in the continued love of their daughter that her presence became more real than those of flesh and blood who surrounded them in the same apartment, or who passed them in the street, but whose faces and names were unknown.

By their lives Billie's parents proved that when love is strong, the memory of an absent loved one is more dear and more real than the reality of those who are present. It is love that confers the gift of continued existence in the mind and heart of the loved one. The memory of another becomes ourselves. When we remember we bring the past into the present and give it life alongside the humdrum routine of every day that forces its realities upon us.

The surest comfort for those who have had a loved one snatched away by the hand of death is this: a firm faith in the real and continual presence of our loved ones; it is the clear and penetrating conviction that death has not destroyed them, nor carried them away. They are not even absent, but living near to us, transfigured; having lost in their glorious change no delicacy of their spirit, no tenderness of their hearts, nor special preference in their affection; on the contrary, having in depth and fervor of devotion grown larger a hundredfold. Death is a translation into light, into power, into greater love.

In a certain respect, your loved ones are closer now than ever before. When they were citizens of the planet Earth, you had to wait until you saw them to speak to them. Now, you may speak to them any moment of the day or night.

Listen to the words of Cardinal Manning: "Let us learn that we can never be lonely or forsaken in this life. Shall they forget us because they are made perfect? Shall they love us less because they now have the power to love us more? No trial can isolate us, no sorrow can cut us off from the communion of saints. The heavenly world hangs serenely overhead; only a thin veil floats between. All whom we loved and all who loved us are ever near."

Several years ago Billie's father died, and the following year, her mother. Although her parents were desperately poor in this Earth's goods, they were rich in the blessing of having such a lovely girl to lead them to God.